ALSO BY JOE POSNANSKI

Paterno

The Machine

The Soul of Baseball

The SECRET
of GOLF

THE STORY OF TOM WATSON
AND JACK NICKLAUS

JOE POSNANSKI

SIMON & SCHUSTER

New York   London   Toronto   Sydney   New Delhi

Simon & Schuster
1230 Avenue of the Americas
New York, NY 10020

First Simon & Schuster hardcover edition June 2015

SIMON & SCHUSTER and colophon are registered trademarks of Simon & Schuster, Inc.

For information about special discounts for bulk purchases, please contact Simon & Schuster Special Sales at 1-866-506-1949 or business@simonandschuster.com.

The Simon & Schuster Speakers Bureau can bring authors to your live event. For more information or to book an event, contact the Simon & Schuster Speakers Bureau at 1-866-248-3049 or visit our website at www.simonspeakers.com.

Interior design by Ruth Lee-Mui

Manufactured in the United States of America

1   3   5   7   9   10   8   6   4   2

Library of Congress Cataloging-in-Publication Data

Posnanski, Joe.
The secret of golf : the story of Tom Watson and Jack Nicklaus / Joe Posnanski.
    pages   cm
Includes bibliographical references.
1. Watson, Tom, 1949–   2. Nicklaus, Jack.   3. Golf—United States—History.   4. Golfers—United States—Biography.   5. Sports rivalries.   I. Title.
GV964.A1P67   2015
796.3520922—dc23   2015007266

ISBN 978-1-4767-6643-0
ISBN 978-1-4767-6645-4 (ebook)

For Margo, Elizabeth, and Katie

For Margo, Elizabeth, and Katie

The SECRET *of* GOLF

HITTING ON THE RANGE

Ben Hogan found the secret first. The other golfers of the time looked at Hogan with a mixture of wonder and pity. He practiced golf. He practiced swinging a golf club mornings, afternoons, evenings, and well into darkness. He practiced until his hands bled, until hard scabs formed, and then until they bled again. Years later, when people talked about how much Hogan suffered for his craft, he corrected them. "I did not suffer," he told them. "I loved it all." How could he explain this? Hogan loved to practice more than he loved playing the game itself.

Why? Hogan was a haunted man. His father had committed suicide when Ben was nine; many would believe that Chester Hogan shot himself while young Ben watched. Hogan never said anything about that. He became famous for being remote.

Though he played golf in front of crowds, he always seemed alone. In Scotland they called him the Wee Ice Mon.

One story: At the Masters in 1947, Hogan's playing partner, and one of his closest friends on tour, Claude Harmon, made a hole-in-one at Augusta National's famous 12th hole. Hogan made a birdie on the same hole. After Harmon absorbed all the raucous cheers from the crowd, he noticed Hogan doing an unusual thing: walking over to say something. This had never happened before. "Finally," Harmon thought, "Ben Hogan is going to congratulate me and tell me I hit a nice shot."

Hogan took a drag from his cigarette, flicked it away, and said, "You know, Claude, I can't remember the last time I made a birdie on that hole."

Until Ben Hogan came along, the goal of professional golfers was to make it all look as easy as possible. Many were hustlers, con men, gamblers, who made the bulk of their living at country clubs, where they coaxed rich amateur golfers into believing that they never practiced. The most admired professional golfer was Walter Hagen, a man who would drink and carouse all night and play breathtaking golf the next day. His motto: "Don't hurry, don't worry, you're only here for a short visit. So don't forget to stop and smell the roses."

The best players of Hogan's time—Sam Snead, Gene Sarazen, and especially Byron Nelson—followed Hagen's path. They played golf for money and practiced as little as possible. It was Nelson in particular, with his glorious and unvarying swing, who baffled Hogan. He was a great player, but Hogan believed that with effort he could be better. "He's too lazy to practice," Hogan said.

Nelson responded, "Tell Ben I already learned how to swing a golf club."

Nelson and others simply did not get what Hogan wanted.

He was good enough to play golf for money. What was all the practice about? Then, in late 1947, the year he turned thirty-five, Hogan found what he had been seeking. He found a secret. He had been a good golfer. After he stumbled upon the secret, he would grow into an almost mythical figure.

What did he find that day? People still ask. All anyone can say for sure is that after learning this secret, Hogan hit every drive down the middle of the fairway. His approach shots all danced around the hole. Golf, like life, is unconquerable, and yet Hogan never missed. He won his first U.S. Open in 1948, and he won nine other tournaments.

In early 1949, Hogan was almost killed after a head-on collision with a Greyhound bus. The secret, he would say, inspired his recovery. Sixteen months after the crash, though he still had difficulty walking, he returned to play in the U.S. Open. He won. It was the biggest sports story of 1951. A year later, he won the Masters and the U.S. Open. Then, in 1953, he won the Masters, the U.S. Open, and the British Open. Up to that moment the greatest achievement in golf history had been Bobby Jones's Grand Slam (all four majors in one year) of 1930: the U.S. and British Opens and the U.S. and British Amateur Championships. In many ways, Hogan's feat was even more remarkable. New York threw him a ticker-tape parade.

"We are proud of you not only as a great competitor and master of your craft," President Eisenhower wrote in a telegram handed to Hogan as the parade began, "but also as an envoy extraordinary in the business of building friendship for America."

Hogan looked exhausted. His wife said he had lost twenty pounds. He told the assembled press that he was happy with his achievement, but he was ready to get back to practice.

Over the years, Hogan developed an aura, becoming the

closest thing in golf to a holy man. In his later years, his ability to putt a golf ball into the hole abandoned him. He grew so spooked by his putting troubles that he would stand over a putt, frozen as a statue, as if unable even to pull back the club. But he continued to hit his woods and irons purely well into his sixties. The secret he had discovered in 1947 sustained him. When he practiced, crowds formed around him, and in those crowds were other professional golfers trying to learn what only he knew.

What did Hogan find in 1947? He called it "the Secret." Well, at first he called it *a* secret, but over time it became *the Secret*. Golfers everywhere had to know what it was; it became something of a national obsession. In 1953 *Golf Digest* wrote a story titled "Hogan's Secret," which claimed that the key to his staggering consistency was a twenty-minute training routine that involved hitting golf balls with his feet clamped together as if he were bound by rope and about to be thrown onto railroad tracks. Many golfers tried the program; their shots still sprayed left and right.

On April 5, 1954, the cover of *Life* magazine featured saguaro cactuses at sunset. The main headline, "The World We Live in (Part VI): The Desert," was in the top right-hand corner. Below that, in only slightly smaller letters, was another headline: "Ben Hogan's Secret: A Debate."

"I have a secret," Hogan was quoted as saying. "It's easy to see if I tell you where to look."

In *Life* that week, seven golf experts tried to unravel the Secret. The PGA champion Walter Burkemo theorized that Hogan's trick was that he "drops his hands at the top of the backswing." Claude Harmon guessed the key had something to do with the lack of rotation of Hogan's body as he swung: "Hogan's body doesn't turn, it just slides forward." Sam Snead, Hogan's greatest rival, believed the whole Secret thing was nonsense, but he took a guess anyway and said Hogan hit the ball straight every time because his hands never crossed during the swing. These guesses sent golfers across America scurrying to the practice range to try out the possibilities. And golf scores across the country stayed exactly where they had been.

A few months later, Hogan himself graced the cover of *Life* magazine. The headline: "Ben Hogan Tells His Secret." He was reportedly paid $10,000—more than twice the median income of families in 1954—to divulge the Secret. He explained that the thing he had discovered on the practice range that day in 1947 was something old Scottish golfers called "pronation." This involved bending his left wrist backward at the top of the backswing after making a slight grip change.

Almost immediately, people were convinced that Hogan was holding out. Pronation? This could not be the real Secret. People tried the pronation thing, and if anything they found their slices drifting farther to the right and their snap hooks burying deeper in the bushes. Golfers tried changing their grips, tried bending their wrists more, tried pronating all they could. Their golf didn't get any better. This was no secret.

Funny thing: the pronation letdown did not dampen golfers' enthusiasm; instead it convinced them that Hogan was keeping the true Secret to himself. Many of Hogan's friends revealed that he had told them (and them alone) the true Secret, but their versions were no more fulfilling or helpful than pronation. Hogan once told the golfer Ben Crenshaw that the Secret was to hit the ball on the second groove of the clubface. What kind of secret was that? It was like telling a baseball hitter that the way to hit home runs is to hit the ball on the ninth stitch or telling an aspiring superhero that the secret to flight is to fly above the ground.

Hogan himself hinted through the years that, yes, he did keep the real Secret to himself. Snead famously said, "Anybody can say he's got a secret if he won't tell what it is." In his compelling book *Hogan*, Curt Sampson quotes *Golf Magazine* editor Jim Frank as saying, "I always had the feeling he was laughing at us."

But many golfers—countless golfers—believed. The story of Hogan transforming, almost overnight, inspired a new generation of golfers to practice compulsively, ten or twelve hours a day, searching for that formula that would solve the riddle of golf.

One of those true believers was a freckled kid from Kansas City with a fast swing, a gap-toothed smile, and a tendency to splatter golf balls into sand traps and high grass. He would go to the practice range and hit golf balls for so many hours that, like Hogan, he inspired curious looks from other golfers. After Tom Watson read about Hogan he said, "His purpose really became all-consuming. I was drawn to that."

Watson met Hogan only once, and many years later he did not remember much about the meeting. By then Hogan's remoteness had grown into something more; he became a recluse. He gave no interviews. He almost never made public appearances. Sometimes people would see him around Fort Worth, and they would inevitably ask if he would whisper to them the true Secret.

And Hogan, if he was in the mood to say anything, would take a drag of his cigarette and say, "It's in the dirt. Go dig it up for yourself."

EVERY SHOT MATTERS

One of the big differences between amateur and pro golfers is how we practice. I see amateurs out on the driving range just hitting golf balls one after another without thinking. All they're doing is ingraining bad habits. It drives me crazy to see that. Every shot you hit should matter. Every shot you hit should have a purpose. Ask yourself: "Why am I here?"

TOM WATSON

Tom Watson believes this: The point of playing golf is playing golf well. He does not accept any counterargument. Over the years, I have said to him, "Look, some people just want to play golf for fun. They don't care what they shoot. They just want to be out there, in the sunshine, among the trees, walking around with friends and a beer and . . ."

At this point, Watson will cut me off and bark, "It's no fun shooting a lousy score."

This is Watson's core conviction. No, he does not think every amateur can be a great golfer, but he does think every amateur can be a better golfer with a little guidance, a little work, and, most important, a shift in ambition. Many times I have watched him react when people ask him how much they should practice to improve their game. He grins that tight grin of his, the one that reflects not joy but some other elusive emotion, and the man who practiced as much as any golfer since Hogan says, "You determine that. But I'll bet it's more than you practice now."

Late in his life, in 2014, Watson was asked to captain the U.S. Ryder Cup team for the second time. The first time, twenty-one years earlier, the team won a stirring victory over Europe; this time things went wrong. Watson was a sixty-five-year-old golf legend, grumpy, stubborn, and hungry to win in a way that might be considered unseemly to younger players. And the players on the team were young, rich, successful, and perhaps a little bit satisfied. The Ryder Cup, after all, is a golf exhibition between players from the United States and players from Europe. It is only as important as the players make it.

On the Saturday night before the final day of matches, the U.S. team always has a party for the players and their wives or girlfriends. This should give you an idea of the light atmosphere surrounding the Ryder Cup. The United States trailed by a sizable margin, and Watson was fuming. Several of his moves had backfired. The team had disappointed him. But the Saturday night party is a long-standing tradition, and the players gave Watson a signed replica Ryder Cup trophy. According to various news stories, quoting various anonymous players, Watson horrified everyone by grumping that he did not want the replica. He had come for the real Ryder Cup.

With Watson, it always comes back to that question: Why am I here?

Many years ago, when I wrote a daily column for Watson's hometown newspaper, *The Kansas City Star*, he called to complain about something I had written. Complaints are part of a sportswriter's daily life, of course, but this was an unusual call. Watson did not call to correct something I wrote about golf. He did not even call to criticize the grammar, though he has a well-earned reputation as a grammar scold. No, he called to tell me to stop writing those damned list columns.

I was still a young columnist then, still finding my way, and every week I would write a column filled with lists. The lists could be of anything: "Five rules baseball should change" or "Four reasons why the Masters is better than the U.S. Open" or "Six teams that should change their nicknames." It was a gimmick, filler, but it seemed to me a relatively inoffensive thing. Watson was offended.

He called me at the office. Best I remember I had never had a complete conversation with him before.

"This is Tom Watson," he said. "Let me ask you a question. What do you want to be?"

"I'm sorry?"

"What do you want to be?" he repeated.

At this point, I stammered something.

"Do you want to be great?" he asked, piercing my pauses. "Do you want to be thought of the way the greatest sportswriters are thought of, the way people think about Red Smith and Jim Murray and Frank Deford? Do you want to be loved like they are loved? I think it's a question you need to ask yourself. Why do you do what you do? What's it all about? Do you want to be great? Not enough people ask themselves that question. It's the most important question. It's the only question."

And then he asked me again, "So, do you want to be great?"

There was Watson's question. Ask yourself: Why am I here?

"Yeah," I mumbled. "Yeah, I mean, sure, I want to be great."

"Then stop writing those damned list columns." And he said good-bye and hung up the phone.

HOLE NO. 1

A Scottish golf joke: An American traveled to Scotland to play some golf. The man loved golf, though he lacked the aptitude; he played relentlessly and poorly. He traveled throughout Scotland, all the wonderful old links courses, leaving behind a sad trail of child-size divots and lost golf balls. Finally he came to Turnberry, the famous golf course on the Firth of Clyde in southwestern Scotland. For a golfer there are few landscapes in the world quite like it. As you walk along the firth, the wind tosses and pushes you. Across the water you see Ailsa Craig, a tall rock island where puffins and gannets hover. There are many people, including the course's current owner, Donald Trump, who say Turnberry is the most beautiful golf course on earth.

The American looked at Turnberry with both awe and fear. He hired a caddie and began with an optimistic first drive, then he went about his business of hooking and slicing hopeless shots into gorse bushes and pot bunkers.

"This is how I play," he kept repeating apologetically, and his caddie said nothing at all. Finally, after another of his many hopeless shots, the man asked his caddie, "Any advice?"

The caddie looked up and said, "Ye micht keep yer een oan th' wee baw."

The man played this over in his mind and realized the caddie was saying "You might keep your eyes on the little ball." Well, this struck him as sound advice. Like so many amateurs, he had a habit of taking his eyes off the ball while he swung the club. When he stood over his next shot, he said to himself, "Keep your eyes on the ball. You might keep your eyes on the ball. Ye micht keep yer een oan th' wee baw." Then he began his swing, and it felt different somehow, smoother. At impact he heard a beautiful sound, a gorgeous thump, and he watched awestruck as his drive soared true, splitting the fairway in half. It was the most perfect shot he had ever hit.

The man felt the wind against his face, and he stared out over the land to the stunning Turnberry Hotel in the distance. It was beautiful—green and blue, rolling hills and dunes. He raced after his caddie, who had already started walking, and when they reached the golf ball the man once again told himself, "Ye micht keep yer een oan th' wee baw." Again he felt that smooth swing, heard the invigorating thump of club meeting ball, and watched as the ball floated happily over Wilson's Burn, the stream that protects the flag on the 16th hole. The ball plopped on the green and skipped toward the hole, stopping five feet short.

"Incredible!" the man shouted, and he promptly walked up to his ball, repeated his mantra, and putted it in for a birdie.

"Amazing," he said. "Any more advice?"

The caddie looked up briefly then back at the ground. "Ye micht keep yer een oan th' wee baw," he said again.

Same advice. The man stepped to the 17th, a par-5, and cleared his head of all thoughts except the words of his caddie. Now he said it to himself with a Scottish brogue. *Ye micht keep yer een oan th' wee baw.* His drive was brilliant again, straight and true, and his second shot rolled up close to the green. His chip shot for eagle almost dropped into the hole, and he made his second straight birdie.

"I have to tell you this," he said to the caddie. "I've never made back-to-back birdies in my life. This is amazing. You've cured me."

The caddie shrugged. "Ye micht keep yer een oan th' wee baw," he said again.

On the 18th hole, the man cleared his mind one more time. *Een oan th' baw. Een oan th' baw.* He watched the ball, began the same backswing, and came down with the same swing that had felt so good the previous two holes . . . and this time he snap-hooked his drive so violently that the ball began curving left the instant he hit it. It did not stop curving until it was a hundred yards off-line and lost forever in angry-looking vegetation.

The man shouted to his caddie, "Oh no! Where did that go?"

The caddie shrugged. "Lik' ah tellt ye," the man said. "Th' way ye play golf, ye micht keep yer een oan th' wee baw."

Tom Watson and Jack Nicklaus stood at the 16th tee of Turn-berry that day in 1977, and all around them was chaos. In the gallery, shirtless men the color of pink grapefruit pushed and bumped into each other as they tried to get a view of the two golfers. Normally sensible people could not stop babbling, even after golf marshals pleaded with them for silence. The golf world felt like it was tilting off balance. When it comes to golf, Scottish people are famously reserved, undemonstrative, difficult to impress. Golf is like church in Scotland, church like golf.

That day, though, the final day of what later was called the Duel in the Sun, sunburned Scots skittered around Turnberry like it was Woodstock. They could not stop jumping and chattering and moving. It was the golf Watson and Nicklaus were playing: nobody had ever seen anything quite like it. The men hit gorgeous shot after gorgeous shot, brilliant putt after brilliant putt—it was music, not golf. Years later, a member named Jack Boyd, who would become the unofficial historian of Turnberry, remembered feeling like everyone was walking five feet off the ground. The golf was so heavenly, Boyd said, the Scottish wind dared not blow.

The people of Scotland did not know Tom Watson, not yet. He was the challenger then, the young golfer who dared be king. Watson did not know Scotland either. He did not yet understand why people spoke so reverentially about Scottish links golf. He was a sensible midwesterner raised by sensible midwestern parents to cherish sensible midwestern values. Don't brag. Don't draw attention. Win modestly. Lose with dignity. You get what you deserve. Watson believed this was true of life, and even more, true of golf. He grew up playing the golf of retributive justice.

In links golf, though, that was turned upside down. In links golf, you deserve whatever you get.

Like all links courses, Turnberry is built on rolling dunes that link the land and the sea. Before there was golf, Turnberry looked like a golf course. The golf courses in Kansas City and around the American Midwest, where Watson grew up, are lined with trees, dotted with lakes and traps with fluffy white sand. They are built with bulldozers and shovels. Links courses, the Scots say, are found, not built. They feature few trees and very little water, and the sand traps are holes in the ground. A perfect links golf course looks like it was built by God and untouched by human hands. There's a famous Sam Snead line; he was on a train passing by the Old Course at St. Andrews, the place where golf as we know it began. "Say," Snead said as he looked out the window, "it looks like there used to be a golf course there."

The pride Scottish people have when recounting that story is telling. St. Andrews is the near-perfect essence of links golf. On Sundays at St. Andrews, people walk their dogs on the world's most famous golf course. They ride skateboards on the hard grass. Scottish golf courses have no tricks, no man-made lakes in your path, no planted trees to block the view of flags. Links courses rely on nature to guard the hole. The dunes make golf balls bounce unpredictably. Native grasses and gorse bushes eat golf balls. Golf architects dig small, deep sand bunkers where rabbits once clawed the land, where sheep slept.

And there is the weather. In Scotland they say, "Nae wind, nae rain, nae golf." It is a philosophy, not only of golf but also of life.

All this meant little to the twenty-seven-year-old Tom Watson. He had a specific, even Catholic idea about how golf should be played. Good shots were to be rewarded. Bad shots were to be punished. This was the game his father, Ray Watson, taught him.

So it confounded him that in links golf good shots would sometime bounce erratically and drop into those nasty pot bunkers. Bad shots sometimes would roll through the high grass and prickly plants and settle on a pristine piece of land. The wind often could not be judged; it would gust and bluster and then suddenly fall still. A perfectly struck shot hit into calm air would run into a new wall of wind and get knocked out of the sky like a clay pigeon. The next shot might be turned left by a fresh wind and disappear.

"This is not golf," Watson thought.

•　　•　　•

Watson and Nicklaus stared out toward the Turnberry Hotel in the distance and waited. One of them was going to win the Open Championship; one of them was not. There was no one else left. They had hit so many brilliant shots on the final day that they left the tournament behind. They were each ten shots under par, the lowest scores in the history of the Open Championship (as it is called in Great Britain and around the world—never the British Open). The third-place golfer, Hubert Green, was an impossible nine shots behind.

Watson studied Nicklaus's face. How many times through the years had he studied Nicklaus's face? A hundred? A thousand? Watson hoped there was something revealing there, something that might explain Nicklaus's greatest strength: the way his mind worked when he was under pressure.

Golfers make mistakes—people make mistakes—when a moment grows tense. They make mistakes in judgment, mistakes in tempo, mistakes in strategy. But pressure did not seem to have power over Jack Nicklaus. Pressure clarified his thoughts. Trouble steeled his nerve. Watson watched Nicklaus and thought, "He already knows he's going to win this. He doesn't *think* he's going to win. He *knows* it." Many years later, the golf writer Dan Jenkins would sum up Nicklaus with a similar view: "You can't compare Jack with anyone else. It was almost as if he felt it was his birthright to win major championships."

Nicklaus, for his part, would not remember considering Watson at all. He was not yet curious about him; that would come later. Young challengers rose and faded throughout Nicklaus's career. Lee Trevino, a wisecracking Mexican American who Watson later said was the best ball-striker he ever saw, beat Nicklaus for a time. Johnny Miller's swing was so gorgeous, Nicklaus taught it to his own sons. Tom Weiskopf was tall and angular and hit high, soft shots. Over the years, there were so many "next Nicklauses"—Ben Crenshaw, Ray Floyd, Lanny Wadkins, and John Mahaffey, to name only a few—that at some point Nicklaus stopped distinguishing. They were all young, all talented, and they had all withered when they got too close to the sun. Now there was Watson.

Watson looked positively midwestern. Pale. Freckled. Red hair. Sportswriters compared him to Tom Sawyer or Huckleberry Finn. *The New Yorker*'s Herbert Warren Wind would capture Watson with a single sentence: "It is easy to picture him sucking on a stem of grass as he heads for the fishing hole with a pole over his shoulder."

The thing that amazed other golfers about Watson was his brilliant short game. That is to say, around the green and around the flag, he did magical things. "Tom could chip it out of a garbage can," Nicklaus said later. But Nicklaus still felt sure he would win at Turnberry. He felt sure because he had a symbiotic relationship with pressure: the bigger the moment, the better he played, and the better he played, the bigger the next moment. And Watson? The sportswriters called him a choker. His swing could get erratic at inopportune moments. He had folded under pressure on numerous occasions. He simply did not know the things Nicklaus had learned about winning, about finishing off a tournament, about how to deal with the turbulent feelings a golfer feels when close to victory. The air was thin, as if they were at altitude, and the Scottish gallery was pink and tipsy and alive. This was Nicklaus's time.

At the 16th hole of Turnberry, on the last day of the 1977 British Open, Nicklaus looked over to Watson and saw something he did not expect. Watson did not look nervous at all. He did not seem unsure. He was looking over the buzzing crowd and the

PERFECT
THE GRIP

To learn the game properly, you must have the proper grip. That's the very first thing—how do you hold on to the club? The grip is also the hardest thing to change. I was lucky. Before anything else, my father taught me how to grip a golf club.

TOM WATSON

The secret in golf is elusive. It can change every day. On a Monday, the secret to playing well might be keeping your head straight. On Wednesday, though, the secret might be in how smoothly you take back the club. By Friday, the secret might be watching the ball and not the club when putting. The secret disappears and reappears like a bumblebee in the wind. Always, though, the grip determines a golfer's fate.

Watson believes bad grips are the biggest problem for recreational golfers. He has played in countless pro-ams, tournaments where amateurs play with professionals, and has given thousands of instructional clinics through the years. He has seen every kind of amateur golfer and every kind of bad habit. And he says the vast majority of golfers do not grip the golf club properly. It is perhaps the simplest thing in the game. But then, it is usually the simplest things that trip people up.

Most people have weak grips. This means that when they hit the golf ball, the face of the club is open (facing slightly to the right). Weak grips lead to slices, when the ball spins uncontrollably to the right, turning like a car exiting an American highway. Some golfers have grips that are too strong, meaning that at impact the face of the club is shut (facing to the left). This leads to hooks, often violent ones. The ball will make a sharp left turn. Slices and hooks are both problems, but a slice is easier to live with. Watson loves to quote his friend Lee Trevino, who said, "You can at least talk to a slice. A hook won't listen."

So Watson says that the first thing a golfer should do is develop a good grip. Unfortunately, it takes a lot of effort to break old habits. It takes hours of practice and days of frustration. Is it worth the effort? Golfers all over the world play golf adequately and happily with terrible grips. Watson concedes that's a perfectly reasonable way to play golf. There's only one thing: these players will never get much better.

"Who wants to play golf," he says, "and not get better?"

Watson teaches the grip with four simple points for right-handers; left-handed players will simply reverse the process:

1. Pick up a golf club with your left hand. Remember that it is the nondominant arm that powers the swing.
2. Turn the club in your left hand so that your left thumb goes down the right center of the shaft and not directly over the center. This is a big mistake many people make; they have their thumb go straight down the shaft, which leads to a weak grip and slices. Ray Watson would tell the young Tom to have his hand turned so that he could see two knuckles.

Even after hitting millions of golf balls, Watson still will occasionally look down for those two knuckles before hitting a shot.

3. Overlap the left with the right hand (there are several ways to do this) so that the V between the thumb and index finger on your right hand is pointed at your right shoulder.

4. Grip the club with your fingers, not your palms. This helps with flexibility and control.

This is obviously not a complete lesson on the grip. There are many people who give grip advice; Watson has written several chapters on the subject. The point is to think about the simple things. The secret, Watson says, is to consider and reconsider the basic details, again and again, even as your mind pushes you to more complicated thoughts.

HOLE NO. 2

Sons learn golf from their fathers, but it isn't the golf they re-member best. Moments linger. Scenes endure. Watson remem-bers some of the golf lessons his father taught him, remembers some of the great shots he saw his father hit. More than anything, though, he keeps close the image of Raymond Watson after Tom hit a shot that worked out well. Gary Player says, "You cannot hide from yourself on a golf course. You are your true self."

Ray Watson's true self was hard and demanding and utterly unforgiving. "Lucky shot," he grumbled. "That was nothing but a lucky shot."

Charlie Nicklaus played every game ever invented, and every now and again he would invent a game of his own. "First one to the car wins," he would shout just after he began running. He was a pharmacist, but it seemed everybody in Columbus, Ohio, knew him from one of his many athletic bits of glory. Charlie played football at Ohio State and then went on to play semiprofession-ally. He was a baseball star in high school. He was the best tennis player in the neighborhood. If he saw a game, any game, he would join in, and he would make the games more fun. Charlie Nicklaus was just one of those rare souls who made people happy. Even Woody Hayes, the famously quick tempered Ohio State football coach who was fired after hitting an opposing player, would simmer down when he was around his friend Charlie. "You're right, Charlie," Woody would say after his temper cooled. "You're right."

Charlie picked up golf after wrecking his ankle playing in a neighborhood volleyball match. He could not run, but he could walk, and Mark Twain did call golf a good walk spoiled. He joined the Scioto Country Club, which was a bit north of Columbus. He took his ten-year-old son, Jackie, along. In golf terms, this was like the moment when Leopold Mozart taught his son Wolfgang how to play a minuet. Jackie shot a 51 on the first nine holes he ever played.

When Jack Nicklaus talks about playing golf as a boy with his father, he talks about the fun. It was like playing golf with a buddy. The two poked fun at each other, made crazy bets that neither would ever pay off, tried hard to win, and laughed and hugged when the match was over. When Jackie showed early brilliance for the game, Charlie realized he was out of his depth. He handed over his son to a local pro named Jack Grout, who would hold Jackie's head straight and tell him to hit the golf ball as hard as he could. The ball sailed. Grout would teach Jack Nicklaus for the rest of his life.

Still, Jack would always say that Charlie taught him how to compete. Every round, Jack could count on his father to say something like "If you outdrive me, hit your second shot inside me, make your putt, and I miss my putt, I'll buy you a car." Everything was a competition, but Charlie didn't see this as a negative thing. "There's nothing better, Jackie," he said, "than playing someone who demands the best of you."

"I'm lucky," Jack says now. "My dad was my best friend." This is the picture he would keep fresh in his mind, even after he became the greatest golfer who ever lived, the picture of playing golf with his best friend.

Ray Watson too was likeable but in a more conservative and hard-bitten way. When he was a teenager, he had a beautiful golf swing and a ferocious temper. He was so notorious for his club throwing that once, after a typical outburst, his friends took their golf clubs out of their bags and threw them, one by one, at Ray's legs. He stopped throwing clubs after that, but his fury did not dissipate.

Ray was a successful midwestern insurance broker, and so Tom grew up at the Kansas City Country Club, which often called itself the third-oldest country club west of the Mississippi. In Kansas City it was simply called the Country Club. This was the center of Kansas City society. The Country Club had no Jew-ish members and no black members. The membership was white, midwestern, gray, conservative, successful. It was the inspiration for the club that Mr. and Mrs. Bridge belonged to in Evan Con-nell's Bridge novels—a place for dyed-in-the-wool Republicans to escape into their own world:

> Very seldom did a ballet perform in Kansas City, a situation which Mr. Bridge regarded with profound indifference. He had never been to a ballet, he had never considered going to a bal-let, and when he chanced to notice in the *Star* that a New York company had scheduled two nights in the municipal audito-rium he reflected that they would probably lose money. Not enough people cared for this type of entertainment. He was bemused by the announcement. Whoever was responsible for booking the troupe knew very little about Kansas City.

Ray came from Kansas City royalty. His grandfather, Isaac Newton Watson, was a crusading lawyer during the time the political machine of Boss Tom Pendergast reigned over Kansas City. He gained local fame for helping bring down Boss Tom. Isaac's son became a lawyer as well; he died in a plane crash when Ray was young. As a young man Ray probably had the talent to become a pro golfer, but golf was not a respectable career choice for a Watson. He went to Stanford like his father, studied law, and settled down in insurance. He satisfied his golf thirst by entering amateur tournaments, winning the Country Club championship several times. He set the course record at the club low enough that his son did not break it until long after he turned professional.

The writer Calvin Trillin grew up in a different part of Kansas City a few years behind Ray; he has written that every family has a message, a theme passed along from one generation to the next. The message might be "We endured so you could live a better life" or "Never dishonor the family name." His own father, Abe, passed along a more unpretentious and Jewish message: "You might as well be a mensch."

Ray's message was more to the point: You play life to win. The message lived and breathed in every exchange between father and son, especially on the golf course. No shot Tom ever hit was good enough. No achievement ever satisfied. If Jack Nicklaus's lasting memory is of his father hitting a funny shot, laughing about it, putting his arm around his son, Tom Watson's memory is of trying and inevitably failing to beat his father. He would hear his old man say to his friends, "He will never beat me." They had a standing bet: if Tom won, he would get paid, but if he lost he had to prune his father's rosebushes. Tom remembered a childhood of rosebushes and frustration. If he wanted to beat his father at this game, he would need to find something inside himself.

Young Tom Watson, like the young Jack Nicklaus, showed promise in the game. When Watson was six, he hit golf balls with a cut-down mashie (something like a 6-iron) that Ray had special ordered from Scotland. Stan Thirsk, the Kansas City Country Club pro who would become Watson's lifelong teacher, could close his eyes sixty years later and still see that six-year-old boy swinging the golf club exactly like his father: "Tom always knew how to imitate others. So he simply imitated his dad."

Watson won some youth tournaments and showed enough promise that people around the Midwest began to talk about him. He could hit the golf ball high and far, and he had a surgeon's touch around the greens. Still, he wasn't the young phenom Nicklaus had been. Nicklaus won his first Ohio State Junior title when he was twelve. He won the Tri-State High School title before he was in high school. He qualified for the U.S. Amateur when he was sixteen and beat professionals at the Ohio Open that same year.

Watson's success was more local. He won four Missouri state amateur titles. But his pinnacle happened with almost no one watching, at Walloon Lake Country Club in northern Michigan. It was 1963, four months before John Kennedy was assassinated, and Watson was thirteen. He and his family spent a month every summer at Walloon Lake. That day Tom and Ray were playing in the final round of the club championship. Tom led going into the 18th hole. He felt sure this would be the time he finally beat his father. Ray, though, evened the match with a touch of inspired, ingenious golf. On the first extra hole, Ray needed a twelve-foot putt to keep the match alive. He dropped the putt. Ray Watson would not lose easily.

On the next hole, Tom hit his second shot safely on the green about thirty-five feet away from the hole. Ray missed the green entirely. His ball landed in a tough spot, and it seemed unlikely that he could get up and down. Tom's moment seemed to have arrived. Even many years later, he remembered how intently his father looked over his shot and considered every possibility. There wasn't a word spoken. Then Ray hit a beautiful little chip shot that rolled to within a couple of feet of the hole.

Tom felt the disappointment growl in his stomach. He now had to make his long putt to win. He studied the putt and clearly saw the line to the hole. He rapped the ball toward the hole, and it stopped about eighteen inches short. He looked at the ball in shock. He never left his putts short. He chalked it up to nerves and waited for his father to concede the short putt so they could go on to the next hole. Conceding short putts is one of the hallmarks of match play in golf.

But there was silence. Tom looked up at his father, and he would never forget the look on his face. He just glared at his son. He would not concede this putt. When Tom looked again at the ball, the eighteen-inch putt suddenly looked more like three feet. When he looked again, the three feet had stretched to five. He glanced once more at his father, almost pleading, and saw the same hard look. In that look, Tom Watson heard the lesson: "Make it yourself. You play life to win."

Tom stepped over the ball and missed the putt. Then he shook his father's hand in defeat. He had learned just how much winning meant.

"That," Ray would tell friends with a mixture of pride and chagrin, "was the last time I beat Tom."

THE LIE

The first thing you look at is the lie. The lie tells you what to do.

TOM WATSON

Golfers, even the best golfers, tend to think simple thoughts. It is a misconception many of us have about successful people in all fields, from the best writers to surgeons to physicists, that they are lost in complications, pondering thoughts that would stagger our minds. At times, that's probably true, but much of what successful people think about is relentlessly simple, building blocks that lead to the complex things.

So it is with golfers. When people ask Watson for advice, they usually want to know about some of the most difficult shots: how to make golf balls hold against the wind, how to hit high shots that stop quickly, how to hit long bunker shots. Watson, of course, has answers, but these are no more useful for an average golfer than if the cinematographer Emmanuel Lubezki tried to explain elaborate lighting concepts to a parent filming his daughter's soccer game. Watson says that the secrets Nicklaus and Hogan and Byron Nelson know are not magical things only professionals can do. They are mundane, common things they always do, time after time, swing after swing, without fail.

The first and most basic of those is to consider how the golf ball lies.

Many amateur golfers settle on what shot they will hit before they even get to their golf ball. If the ball is in the fairway, they calculate the distance to the green and choose their club accordingly. If the ball is in the rough, they choose a club that should get the ball out and closer to the green. Most of us see golf as a two-dimensional sport, the ball being at Point A, the flag at Point B.

Watson's game is three-dimensional. His Point A is not *where* the ball lies but *how* it lies. Is it buried in the grass or settled comfortably on top of it? Is it against the grain of the grass or with it? Is it above his feet or below? On hard or soft ground? If the ball is in a bunker, the lie matters even more: Is it on an uphill lie? A downhill lie? Is it plugged deep in the sand? Resting on top? The lie serves as his instruction manual. It tells him what to do.

"I see amateur players all the time who don't even look at their lie before deciding how to hit their next shot," Watson says. He says this is like a landscape architect making plans without looking at the plot of land or a baseball pitcher winding up and throwing without considering the stance and skill level of the batter.

"The lie is everything." With a bad lie, even the most basic shots require adjustments. With a good lie, the most miraculous shots are possible. Watson's longtime caddie, Bruce Edwards, shouted out the same little prayer every time Watson hit a shot off-line: "He would say, 'Just give us a swing.' That was all we ever needed. 'Give us a good lie. Give us a swing.' He would always say that if I had a full swing I could do anything with the golf ball. And he was pretty much right."

And with a bad lie? "You take your medicine. I can't tell you how many times I've seen golfers turn a bad lie into a triple or quadruple bogey. They try to hit what we call hero shots, and it almost never turns out well. Take your medicine. Chip out. Give yourself a swing. The lie will tell you what to do, but you have to listen. People have to realize that sometimes the golf course wins."

HOLE NO. 3

Watson's hero was Arnold Palmer. There were other golfers to admire. Sam Snead was his father's idol. Well into his sixties Snead had the game's most gorgeous swing. Ben Hogan almost died in a car wreck the year Watson was born, and his comeback and meticulous brilliance dominated golf coverage while Watson was growing up. And there was the young Jack Nicklaus, who emerged on the pro golf scene when Watson was ten with a game that seemed quantifiably bigger than anyone else's.

But to Watson, Palmer was the ideal. Everything about the way Palmer played golf spoke to him. Palmer was bold and dashing, as much Hollywood star as golfing star. "The television camera loved him," CBS's pioneering television producer Frank Chirkinian said. "Arnold would show up on the screen and it was like, 'Wham!' Electric! Nobody thought golf could be exciting on television. He made it exciting."

Palmer came from the small Pennsylvania town of Latrobe (he grew up with television's Mister Rogers) and, like Watson and Nicklaus, had been taught the game by his father. Deacon Palmer was the head pro and groundskeeper at the Latrobe

Country Club. His son's swing dispensed with grace; he reared back, slashed at the ball, and twirled the club at the end. Then he would smoke a cigarette and walk a gunslinger's walk toward the green, where he made putts from everywhere. They called Palmer "the King," and huge galleries known as "Arnie's Army" followed him and cheered for him and prayed for him.

When Watson was fifteen, he was an accomplished enough golfer, having won the Kansas City Amateur the year before, that his teacher, Stan Thirsk, was able to set up an exhibition match between him and Palmer. Watson could not sleep the night before. When he saw the King up close for the first time, he could not believe how big Palmer's arms were and how power seemed to radiate off him.

Introductions were made. Watson stepped to the tee first. He wanted to make an impression. He was fifteen years old, unsure about where his life was headed, but he wanted to be sure Arnold Palmer remembered him. He stepped to the tee and smashed the most overwhelming drive of his young life, a blast that flew almost three hundred yards.

Watson bent down to pick up his tee, and then he looked up at Palmer. He never forgot the King's reaction. Palmer's eyes widened a bit. Then a small smile curled on his lips: so this was how it was going to be. He stepped to the tee with every eye on him and unleashed his drive—about twenty yards beyond Watson's.

"That was Arnie," Watson would say. "That was my hero."

By the time Watson and Palmer played their little exhibition in Kansas City—Palmer won with a good back nine—time was turning against the King. Jack Nicklaus had arrived. He was blond and chubby—they called him "Fat Jack"—and utterly calculating. It was this last part that exasperated Watson. Palmer went for daring and valiant shots time after time. Nicklaus, even as a young man, played more sensibly. "I hated Jack," Watson later admitted.

He was hardly alone. Almost nobody liked Nicklaus in his younger days. Nobody approved of his colorless but devastating game or his unmistakable ambition to take the throne from Palmer. Nicklaus's greatness seemed to come too easily to him. Watson remembered that when he was six, his father told him that a sixteen-year-old golfer named Jack Nicklaus had beaten all the pros at the Ohio Open. Not long after, Nicklaus won two U.S. Amateurs, and at twenty he finished second at the U.S. Open. He played with Ben Hogan that day, and Hogan's famous quote—"I played with a kid who would have won this thing by ten shots if he knew what he was doing"—perfectly described the overwhelming talent Nicklaus displayed with seemingly no effort at all.

When Nicklaus announced he was turning professional in late 1961, Palmer's days as the world's best player were dwindling. Palmer's verve, his competitive fury and magical putting stroke simply could not overtake Nicklaus's overwhelming shots, mathematical mind, and breathtaking confidence. No golfer had ever hit drives so far and straight; no golfer had ever hit iron shots so high; and no golfer had ever seemed so sure that everyone else was playing for second place.

"Young man," Charlie Nicklaus's hero Bobby Jones said to Jack, "you play a game I am unfamiliar with."

Palmer fans, Watson among them, found Nicklaus's rise (and Palmer's inevitable fall) unacceptable. Nicklaus might play great golf, but he was bland and cool, and on television he looked plump and unheroic. Golf needed James Bond on top of the game, not a James Bond villain. At tournaments, Arnie's Army hounded Nicklaus, taunted him after wayward shots, cheered his misses. Watson found this treatment distasteful—golf was supposed to be a gentleman's game—but he quietly rooted for Palmer to suppress the young challenger's insurrection and win back his throne. "Jack was just a villain," Watson remembered. "He had taken over Arnie's kingdom."

When Watson was seventeen, a little over a year after playing with Palmer, he was paired up with Nicklaus in an exhibition in Topeka, Kansas. It would be overly dramatic and wrong to say the day foreshadowed their great duels to come: they both played lousy. The crowd was subdued. It was a cold and dreary day; there was none of the crackling energy of the Watson-Palmer match-up. Watson's enduring memory is of popping up his first drive and the ball going maybe 150 yards, about half the distance of his first shot against Palmer. Nicklaus remembered that he putted about as poorly as he ever had in his life. The rest of the exhibition was unmemorable. They each shot 2-over par 74s.

But playing side by side with Nicklaus had an impact on Watson. When the exhibition ended, Watson told his teacher, Thirsk, that he wanted to refine his upright swing so it was more like Nicklaus's. He loved Palmer, but after seeing Nicklaus's power and precision up close, he knew that there was a new way to play golf.

Watson went to Stanford because his father had gone to Stanford, just as Ray went to Stanford because his father had. It wasn't something Tom remembered thinking about much.

Later in life, his friends would say that certainty was Watson's defining principle. "Tom's not always right, but he's always sure" is how his agent Chuck Rubin described him. But when Watson headed to college, he felt himself drifting. He was not certain about anything at all, even his golf. He did not get a golf scholarship to Stanford and, at first, was not even sure he would play for the golf team. The team's coach, Bud Finger, had to ask him to try out. Watson did not know what he wanted to do or who he wanted to be. He did not even have a major in mind. He took a psychology class, where the teacher handed out envelopes containing personality reports the school had put together based on each student's records and class work. The students were told to write a paper agreeing or disagreeing with their report's findings. Almost everyone in the class agreed with his or her personal report, only to find out that the reports were not personalized at all. They were all the same. Watson liked that experiment, so he became a psychology major. He never intended to become a psychologist.

"I really had this fear of 'What the heck am I going to do with my life?'" Watson remembers. "I guess most young people have that fear, but I really didn't know. I didn't want to go into business. I never really thought about psychology. I wanted to play golf, but I honestly didn't know if I was good enough."

Stanford intimidated and thrilled him. He felt out of place, and he felt challenged. Much later he would talk about being unhappy at Stanford, a midwesterner who felt out of place in a 1960s hotbed of liberalism, but in many of his early interviews as a professional he talked about how much the school had changed him. In one of the first papers he wrote, he defended the Vietnam War (his father's position), and when his professor challenged him with counterarguments, Watson reconsidered. It was often reported in the 1970s that he marched in anti-Vietnam demonstrations, which he insists wasn't true. But he was certainly caught up in the movement. In the 1972 presidential election, he voted for the antiwar Democrat George McGovern over Richard Nixon, much to his later embarrassment. "You're an idiot," his father told him. "He was right," a sixty-five-year-old Watson conceded.

Watson's golf at Stanford drifted too. He had shown promise as a high school golfer, but at Stanford he never won a major amateur event or an NCAA title. He was never a first-team All-American. His game was brilliant but erratic. When he was a senior, he played in Tucson against a freshman named Gary Koch in the NCAA Championship.

"He was going along in classic Tom style," Koch remembered years later. "You know, he was hitting driver on every hole, trying to make every putt from everywhere on the green. He's playing really well. So we go to the thirteenth hole, it's a short hole. You can hit an iron off the tee. You certainly will hit less than a driver. There's out of bounds on the left, water on the right. There's no way you hit driver there. So Tom goes for his driver.

"And he hits the ball out of bounds, way left. It was just a terrible shot, one no good player would ever try. So what does he do? Well, he takes another ball, and he hits another driver. He hit it out of bounds again. He ends up making an eight on the hole. But the thing I remember most was that he never got angry or frustrated. It was like, 'What are you going to do? This is the way I play.'"

Watson nods when he hears the story. "I had no idea where the ball was going," he admits. "I knew I could hit it far. And I knew I could putt. I had no idea if that was enough."

Watson decided to turn pro on a starry night in his senior year. He was playing golf on the Stanford course late into the afternoon. The sky grayed and then darkened without his noticing. It wasn't until he reached the 11th green (he always remembered the precise hole) that he looked up. There were stars everywhere.

He looked down and realized he could not see his ball. He looked up again at all those stars. He was standing in darkness. No one else was on the course. That was the moment Tom Watson made the prudent decision to try professional golf.

This was how his mind worked. He had played golf in the dark before. He had always practiced with an almost religious zeal; his teacher Thirsk remembered him hitting ball after ball from a little wooden shelter out into the Kansas City snow. He played the Stanford course every Monday through Friday. On Saturdays he woke up at 5 a.m. and drove to one of America's most famous golf courses, Pebble Beach. He arrived so early and so enthusiastically that the starter let him play the course for free before anyone else arrived. He stayed the entire day, and after everyone left, he was allowed to play the course again in the dark. On those days at Pebble Beach, he pretended to be facing Jack Nicklaus at the U.S. Open.

In other words, that starry night was no different from a hundred other starry nights when he was the last one on the golf course. But something about that night unlocked Watson's ordered mind. He looked at those stars and had three clear thoughts:

1. I'm a college senior who doesn't know what to do with my life.
2. I'm out here by myself playing golf in the dark again.
3. Anyone who plays golf in the dark every night should try playing golf for a living.

He had made his choice. Now his biggest worry was telling his father.

He came home during a break, and they went on a hunting trip together. When he thought the moment was right he made his announcement: "Dad, I'm going to become a professional golfer. I don't know if I'm good enough, but I promise you I will work harder than anyone out there."

Ray Watson was a hard man. He did not praise, he did not encourage, and he did not have any use at all for irresponsible dreaming. But that day, Ray looked at his son and said, "That's the right thing to do. If you don't make that decision you will wonder for the rest of your life whether or not you could have made it."

With that Ray and a few of his friends raised enough money to fund Tom on the PGA Tour for two years. That was long enough to see if he could make a living playing golf, his only goal at that point. The thought of becoming a great player came much later.

STUDY BETTER PLAYERS

I would play with old pros in Kansas City all the time, and so I asked each one of them separately one question when I decided to turn pro. I said, "What's the one thing I should do? What's the one thing that will make me a better player?" Each one of them said the same damn thing. They said, "Go play and watch the best players out there."

TOM WATSON

Watson says that he played better after watching Byron Nelson swing a golf club. Nelson had been one of the game's greatest players; he still had a beautiful golf swing well into his sixties and seventies, when Watson got to know him. Nelson's swing was so efficient and dependable that when a man named George Manning built a machine in 1966 that repeated a swing precisely every time, he called it "Iron Byron."

Watson did not consciously learn when he watched Nelson swing. That is to say, he did not watch Nelson swing the club and think, "He keeps his head steady. I need to do that" or "He has a perfect rhythm on his takeaway. I need to bring that to my own game." Instead he appreciated the concise beauty, the pendulum-like wonder, and it felt like a tiny piece of Nelson's talent and skill would magically suffuse him and transfer into his own swing.

But there was nothing magical about it. Watson understood that seeing Nelson swing the club—elegantly, proficiently—altered his own swing. He rarely could put words to those alterations. It was like his body understood. Watching a master at work can have a powerful effect. That is one of the reasons why so many golfers watch weekend golf on television.

So this was one way that watching great players inspired Watson, but it was not the most important way. Those old Kansas City pros that he idolized wanted him to study the thought patterns of the best players and learn how golf should be played. This meant watching Nicklaus. Watson did not love Nicklaus's swing the way he loved Nelson's and Snead's. Nicklaus had flaws. For one, there was his famous flying elbow; he did not tuck in his right elbow on the backswing, which is what golfers were taught to do, but instead let it fly back the way a baseball player holds a bat before swinging. Many thought that would wreck Nicklaus's career. Every time he went into even a mild slump, story after story about his flying elbow would appear. Beyond that, his swing lacked grace. Nelson's swing was art. Nicklaus's was powerful and athletic and brutally effective.

Watson had questions about Nicklaus's play: Why did he hit *that* shot? Why did he use *that* club? Why didn't he go for birdie? What Watson noticed most was how often Nicklaus would hit conservative shots. This was exactly the thing that turned him off as a youngster, when he preferred the risk-taking brilliance of Palmer. But once he reached the PGA Tour, he saw golf—and Nicklaus—in a whole different way.

Nicklaus told him, "More golfers lose golf tournaments than win them."

This fascinated Watson. Nicklaus was not thinking about great shots most of the time; he was thinking about avoiding big mistakes. It seemed counterintuitive to Watson; he had always played the game fast and loose and full of aggression. But watching Nicklaus changed the way he thought. He began to take fewer chances. He began to look for the widest part of the fairway and aim for it. He hit away from bunkers. He would try for the heroic shot only when none of the safer options made sense.

"No golfer hit the right shot more often than Jack Nicklaus," Watson would say, and yes, again, that's the secret of golf.

HOLE NO. 4

While Watson was at Stanford mustering the courage to try professional golf, Nicklaus began, for the first time in his life, to lose interest. Nobody had worked harder at the game than he, and success had come quickly, first as an amateur golfer, then after turning pro. He was twenty-two when he won his first U.S. Open, in 1962, his first professional victory. It had taken Hogan a decade to win his first U.S. Open; Snead never won one. Soon after, Nicklaus won the Masters and the PGA Championship.

Palmer's passionate fans held on to their illusions for a while, but the most realistic of them, including Watson, understood that in time Nicklaus would surpass him. The crossing point came on the third day of the 1965 Masters. Palmer was thirty-five and still at the peak of his powers. Nicklaus was twenty-five and just coming into his own. The men were tied, and Arnie's Army marched after them, prepared to cheer every good shot of their hero and every mistake of his nemesis. By the end of the day, though, there were no illusions left. Nicklaus played superb, nearly perfect golf and left Palmer and everyone else in his wake. He would go on to set a Masters record score while Palmer coughed and wheezed to the finish six shots back. Palmer was like a 1950s aircraft that broke the speed of sound; Nicklaus was like one of those new rockets headed for the moon. Their rivalry as golfers was over.

Well, all rivalries were over. Nicklaus stood alone. He won two more major championships in 1966, including his first Open Championship, and the next year set the U.S. Open record for low score at Baltusrol Golf Club in New Jersey. That performance at Baltusrol left Palmer fans reeling. Nicklaus and Palmer were tied on the weekend, and again Nicklaus unveiled sublime golf that Palmer could not counter.

When the match ended, ABC's Jim McKay pulled Palmer aside and tried to get him to comment on some of the amazing shots Nicklaus made that day. While highlights of Nicklaus played on a screen nearby, the normally media friendly Palmer said, "I've looked at this all day. I think I'm going to excuse myself and go to Latrobe."

There seemed no worlds left for Nicklaus to conquer. He was the best golfer in the world, and even before he turned thirty, golf writers wondered if he was the best ever. But now, for the first time in his life, he was losing interest in golf. He had enough money. He had won all the big championships. He had a young family at home.

"When I first came on tour," Nicklaus recalls, "I wanted to win more than anything. I think that probably had something to do with why Arnold's fans disliked me—I wasn't in awe of Arnold. I liked him. But I expected to beat him. I expected to beat everyone." Without Palmer to challenge him, Nicklaus's youthful hunger faded. In 1968, for the first time since he turned pro, he went an entire year without winning a major championship. He finished second at both the U.S. Open and the Open Championship, but he did not give himself a good chance to win either. In 1969 he again went winless in the major championships; he didn't even have a top-five finish. He still won a half-dozen tournaments; he finished second in prize money in 1968 and third the next year. But by this time Nicklaus wasn't much interested in regular tournaments or prize money. He was playing for history. And, for a time, he wasn't much interested in history either.

"I had always worked as hard as anyone," he says. "I really did stop working hard. . . . Other things took my interest."

Two things revived Nicklaus. The first happened at the 1969 Ryder Cup, which was then a team competition between the United States and Great Britain. (It now matches the United States against Europe.) The Ryder Cup was intended to be a gentlemanly competition between passionate golfing nations, but that year it took on an intensity that troubled many golfers. Gamesmanship abounded. The competition was tied going into the final match, where Nicklaus was facing Britain's Tony Jacklin. Their match was all square going into the final hole, and the pressure was overwhelming Jacklin.

"How do you feel, Tony?" Nicklaus asked him as they walked down the fairway.

"Bloody awful," Jacklin answered.

They both put their approach shots on the green. Nicklaus made a testy four-foot putt for par. That left Jacklin with a slightly shorter putt to tie the match and tie the Ryder Cup. Without hesitation, Nicklaus conceded the putt and put his arm around Jacklin. "I don't think you would have missed that putt, Tony," he said. "But I wasn't about to give you the chance."

That act of sportsmanship would become a part of golf lore. But it was on the plane ride home that Nicklaus came to grips with something: he felt tired. He had played poorly on the last day, losing his first match and playing shoddily against Jacklin, and he attributed it to being in lousy shape. For years people had been making Fat Jack jokes; this from one of America's great sports columnists, the *Los Angeles Times*' Jim Murray, is representative: "If [Nicklaus] gets tired of golf, he can make a living as a department store Santa. . . . Arnold Palmer has a belly like a washboard and a back like a chimney. He flies his own plane. Jack Nicklaus has a front like a pile of old clothes and a back like an unmade bed. He gets any heavier, and he'll have to fly as freight."

Nicklaus had always ignored the jokes, at least in public. But on the flight home, he told his wife, Barbara, that he'd had enough: he was going to lose weight. When he got home, with typical Nicklaus commitment he joined Weight Watchers, began running between holes on the golf course, and dropped twenty pounds in a matter of weeks. He started the new golf season looking like a different person; the "Where's Fat Jack?" headlines filled newspapers in the early part of 1970.

In February 1970 Charlie Nicklaus died of cancer at fifty-six. He had been at an Ohio State football game when he started to feel ill. He tried to put on a brave face for the family, but the doctors had given him three months to live. He lasted three months.

"I felt like I had let him down," Jack said years later. "In a way, I felt like Dad lived for my success on the golf course. I don't think anything made him happier. And for a couple of years, I had not put as much into the game as I should have. Did it change me? I had lost my father and my best friend. Of course it changed me."

To his father, the thing that mattered most was major championships. Nicklaus had felt that way too, and he now intensified his focus and energy to win Masters, U.S. Opens, Open Championships, and PGA Championships. His commitment to winning majors became so all-consuming that in 1974, when the PGA

Tour created a new tournament called the Players Championship, Nicklaus made sure to win it "just in case they decide to call
it a major championship in the future." (He won three of the first
five Players Championships.)

He changed his golfing schedule so that he would be well
rested and peaking when the major tournaments came around.
He played even more conservatively based on his belief that more
golf tournaments are lost than won. And perhaps more than anything, he created an aura that intimidated every golfer in the
world. Jack Nicklaus, everyone knew, played his best golf in the
biggest moments.

"Very few guys love to be in contention," said Roger Maltbie, a
fine professional golfer and later a golf announcer. "Yes, you hear
all the time people say, 'You've got to like the pressure. You've got
to like being in that position.' But I think most of them were fib-
bing. There have been only a few guys who really liked that moment of intense pressure; for the rest of us, it was just something
we had to get through.

"Jack though . . . Jack really enjoyed it. I never saw anyone else
who was quite like that. Jack was having fun. Everyone else was
sweating, trying to get their place in history, trying to accomplish
great things, and Jack was out there for the fun of it. The hotter it
got, the more he liked it. At major championships, on Sundays,
he looked like one of the guys going out on a weekend with a six-
pack of beer. Pressure was his six-pack."

Four months after Charlie died, Nicklaus won the 1970 Open
Championship at St. Andrews. There he made one of golf's most
famous shots. He was in a playoff with Doug Sanders and led by
a stroke going into the final hole, one of the most famous par-4s
in the world. On the tee, he took off his yellow sweater and let
loose a 360-yard drive that actually rolled over the green. It was

breathtaking. He chipped back up, made his birdie, and won. He was back on top of the world.

The next year he finished in the top five at all four major championships. In 1972 he won the Masters and the U.S. Open, threatening to become the first golfer to win the modern Grand Slam. At the British Open, he lost by a shot to Lee Trevino, his primary nemesis for a time. In 1973 Nicklaus won the PGA Championship at Canterbury Golf Club in Cleveland. That gave him fourteen major championships, which moved him one past Charlie's hero, Bobby Jones. There was little doubt in anyone's mind that Nicklaus was the best golfer who ever lived.

This was the Jack Nicklaus who ruled golf when Tom Watson joined the PGA Tour.

"Jack knew he was the best," the writer Dan Jenkins said. "Everyone else knew it too. And everyone else knew that he knew it."

DON'T FEEL PRESSURE

If you don't feel pressure, you won't feel pressure.

TOM WATSON

Here's a question Watson has asked himself repeatedly: What is pressure? The answer seems obvious: pressure is a stressful urgency caused by the weight of a moment or the difficulty of a task. But because handling pressure is such a part of Watson's profession, he has spent a lot of time breaking down what pressure means.

"Pressure," he says with some finality, "happens when you are attempting to achieve something you are not sure you can achieve."

Consider driving your car: When you drive on a quiet road in daylight, you probably do not feel any pressure if you are an experienced driver. This is something you have done countless times. It is something you *know* you can do. There is no fear of failure.

Now, say it's raining. Again, if you are an experienced driver, you probably do not feel much pressure, but you might feel some trepidation. The rain turns to snow. Again you may feel trepidation, but not pressure. Say it's snowing hard and you are in

London, where the traffic is heavy and you're not used to driving on the left side of the road. Add in that you are almost out of gas. And your windshield ices up. Each step away from the familiar takes you a step away from comfort. Each step adds pressure as you become less and less certain you can achieve the objective because you've never done it before.

Perhaps more than any other sport, golf focuses pressure on the player. There are no time constraints, as there are in other sports. Your competitors are not allowed to hinder you, as they are in other sports. The pressure originates in yourself; it builds from doubts. A two-foot putt on the practice green doesn't spark many doubts. A two-foot putt to win a bet or a tournament or the Masters is another thing entirely. Now the mind asks, Can I really do this?

"If you don't feel pressure, you won't feel pressure" is Watson's way of saying that the best way to handle and overcome pressure is to not let it build in the first place. How? Well, that's the secret, isn't it? One way is to think positively. The great golf teacher Harvey Penick, used to demand that his students speak positively at all times. He put it like this: "Never say never and don't say don't."

Watson agrees with this in principle, but he also knows that it's not always possible to avoid negativity. Instead he thinks of a tip he got from Duke Gibson, a Kansas City pro he idolized as a child: "Never hit a shot under pressure that you are not capable of executing." In other words, you will feel doubts; you will feel uncertain. The best way to deal with this is to go back to the things you know. Remember that driving in the snow is mostly like driving in sunshine. Follow the same routine you always follow. Return to the familiar. Do what you know how to do.

At the 1978 Masters, Watson went to the final hole tied with Gary Player. Watson needed a par to force a playoff; a birdie would win. He hooked his drive into the trees on the left side. When he got to the ball and saw his difficult lie, he saw two options:

1. He could hit a draw—a gentle hook from right to left—that would probably end up on the right side of the green, where he would have little chance for birdie but a good chance to save par.
2. He could hit a high cut—a left-to-right shot—that, if he hit it just right, would move toward the hole and give him a chance for a birdie and victory.

The first option was the safer shot. Watson had been hitting draws all week (that's what you do at Augusta) and hitting them well. But in the moment, under golf's most intense pressure, he decided to go for the riskier shot, the one he was not sure he could execute. "That," he would say angrily more than three decades later, "created pressure." He hit a poor shot and left the ball in a nearly impossible spot, fifty feet left of the hole at the bottom of a hill. He bogeyed the hole and lost.

"That was the wrong time to play the shot that I wasn't qualified to play," he says. "It cost me the tournament. But it was a learning experience. They're all learning experiences."

HOLE NO. 5

When young golfers want to turn professional they go to the PGA Tour Qualifying School. The "Q School," as it's known, is not a school at all; there are no classes, no teachers, no recesses. The 1971 Q School involved three grueling tournaments, the last a six-day, 108-hole beast at Palm Beach Gardens, Florida. The players with the twenty-three lowest scores earned a card to play on the PGA Tour, a ticket to a dream.

The 1971 Q School was competitive: 357 players tried to get their PGA Tour card that year—more than ever before—and the group was loaded with accomplished young players. U.S. Amateur champions Lanny Wadkins, Allen Miller, and Bruce Fleisher were trying for their cards, as were the NCAA champion John Mahaffey, the World Cup winner David Graham, and the British Amateur champion Steve Melnyk. All of them would make the PGA Tour and, in time, win tournaments.

Tom Watson wasn't a name then. He was an afterthought in this group of stars. Still, and this was a bit of a paradox, Watson had little doubt that he would play well and get his card. For a young man who had been so unsure about playing golf in college and who questioned his talent at every turn, he had startling confidence at the Q School. In this case, though, he had a plan: if he made no more than two double bogeys in any round, he would get his PGA Tour card. Two double bogeys per round may seem like a lot, but Watson believed he would make enough birdies and eagles to handle big mistakes, as long as he did not make more than two of those big mistakes.

Watson had thought through the plan carefully. He felt sure that he had the power and putting skill to make a lot of birdies. The only thing that could keep him from getting his card was big numbers: double bogeys, triple bogeys, and the like. "I knew I didn't have to be perfect," he said later. "I just had to play smart enough to limit my mistakes." Midway through Q School, he was among the leaders. He had a shaky final day, but he'd played well enough to finish fifth and easily qualify for the PGA Tour.

He then raced to Napa, California, to play in the Kaiser International Open, where again he surprised everyone. He played very well the first two days and found himself in third place heading into the weekend. But he floundered over the weekend, finished twenty-eighth, and took home a $1,065 check for his troubles. His career had begun.

Lee Trevino tells a story about a young Tom Watson. On Wednesdays pro golfers would partner with local amateurs to play in pro-ams. Trevino was the perfect pro-am partner: funny, passionate, irreverent. He would say, "You can make a lot of money in golf; just ask my ex-wives." Trevino's humor came from pain. He grew up poor and never knew his father. He left school at fourteen to caddy and shine shoes and make whatever money he could to help his family. At seventeen, he joined the Marines.

All the while, he taught himself an awkward-looking but

staggeringly effective swing. Trevino had immaculate control of the golf ball. After being discharged from the Marines, he became a teaching pro in El Paso, and he honed his game by playing money matches in the Texas dust. "Pressure," he once said, "is when you play for five dollars a hole with two dollars in your pocket." He improved his game to the point where he qualified for the 1966 U.S. Open. He decided then to play professionally, and he quickly became one of the best players on the PGA Tour. He was the first to beat Nicklaus with regularity.

On the golf course, he chattered nonstop, told jokes, offered tips, engaged the gallery. He once pulled a rubber snake out of his bag at the U.S. Open and tossed it to Nicklaus (who had asked to see it). He was struck by lightning on the golf course, which led to his famous advice to golfers when a lightning storm approaches. "Hold up a 1-iron," he said. "Even God can't hit a 1-iron."

His humor was like that: tinged with his own painful memories. "I don't play golf for fun," he once told a reporter. "It's my business. When the mailman starts delivering mail on his day off, that's when I'll start playing golf for the hell of it." In later years, he and Watson would become close friends and help each other through trying times. When Trevino went through all kinds of financial troubles, Watson set him up with his own agent and brother-in-law, Chuck Rubin.

But when Watson first arrived on tour, Trevino had never heard of him. He was playing in a Wednesday pro-am and was walking quickly to get to the first tee when he noticed Watson standing in a bunker and practicing shots. Trevino stopped for a second to watch. This was unusual; golfers didn't practice on pro-am days. There was nobody else practicing, nobody else in sight. Trevino made a note of it; this kid obviously had some passion for the game.

Trevino played in the pro-am, told his familiar jokes, offered some advice, and five hours later he walked by the practice range again. Watson was still hitting shots out of the same bunker.

Yes, Watson worked. Lord, did he work. He had promised his family and sponsors that he would work harder than anyone on the PGA Tour. He had told his girlfriend Linda Rubin that he was giving himself just five years to make it as a professional golfer. He practiced with such intensity that at first this was the only thing the other golfers noticed about him. To them he was simply that odd, freckled guy who seemed to practice every hour of every day.

In 1973, Watson's second full year on the Tour, a young man named Bruce Edwards came to see him at the Norwood Hills Country Club in St. Louis. Edwards was eighteen, five years younger than Watson, but he seemed younger than that. He was the son of a dentist and had decided to put off college so he could become a caddie on the PGA Tour. Watson happened to be a player without a caddie. Edwards asked for a job. Watson gave him a couple of bucks and said, "Go get me two buckets of balls." In those days, PGA golfers had to pay for their practice balls.

Then, while Edwards watched, Watson hit balls. And he hit balls. And he hit balls. Both remembered it being a hundred degrees and feeling hotter; the humidity in St. Louis is famous and withering. But Watson kept giving Edwards money for water and buckets of golf balls. Edwards became fascinated. Who was this madman? Other golfers came out to the range, hit a few balls, and escaped for some air-conditioning. Watson kept hitting.

"I had never seen anyone who wanted to get better *that* much," Edwards said many years later. "I'm not going to lie, I kept looking for signs that he was about finished. It was really hot. Every time he stopped I would think, 'Okay, he's done.' But he would just say, 'Bruce, can you get me some water and another bucket?' He was probably out there for four or five hours. By the end I thought, 'This guy is going to be a star.' "

Watson didn't expect stardom, not in those early days. He just wanted to feel like he belonged. He was desperately lonely his first couple of years on the PGA Tour. He wanted to marry his high school sweetheart, Linda Rubin, but there were complications. Rubin was Jewish, something that would create tension with Watson's conservative father. And Tom worried about supporting a family as a golfer. He made fair money his first couple years on the Tour, but he did not win a tournament. He shared his worries with his teacher, Stan Thirsk, who told him, "Marry that girl." In July 1973 he did. Two weeks later, Watson was on the practice range in St. Louis.

Watson practiced obsessively to find a golf swing that would hold up. He was developing a reputation among fellow golfers and writers as a player who could put himself in position to win but could not finish the job. He led the 1973 Hawaiian Open going into the final round, but then he shot 75 and got passed by first-time winner John Schlee. "What can I say?" Watson told reporters afterward. "I just played bad. I hope I won't make the same mistakes again."

He did make some of the same mistakes. At the end of 1973, he played in an odd eight-round, two-week tournament called the World Open. The tournament was held in Pinehurst, one of the most famous golf courses in America, and offered a $100,000 payoff to the winner, the largest prize in golf history. In the fifth round, Watson shot a 62 to take a commanding six-shot lead. For many years, Edwards would talk about that extraordinary round as the one that told Watson's destiny. "He was just firing at flags all the way," Edwards told the author John Feinstein for the book *Caddy for Life*. "A lot of guys, they get five-, six-under for the day, they start protecting. All they want to do is make pars and get in without messing up. Tom just wasn't built that way. He felt good, and he just kept on firing."

But Watson followed that sensational round with three lousy ones—76, 76, 77—and fell back into a tie for fourth place. People in the golf world whispered that Watson seemed to be lacking something that great golfers need: the fortitude to finish off tournaments. Six months later, those whispers turned into national headlines.

Johnny Miller tells a story about the young Tom Watson. Many golf observers, Nicklaus among them, believe that Miller was as talented as any golfer ever. He grew up in San Francisco and was a precocious young player, finishing eighth at the U.S. Open when he was just a freshman in college. After that he had to deal with the burden of being called the next Jack Nicklaus.

He did not become the next Nicklaus; the reason was putting. Miller was never a great putter even at his peak, and later in his career, he fought a bloody and losing battle with the putter. But he still won two major championships because nobody hit iron shots closer to the flag. Nicklaus said Miller was the best short-iron player he ever saw.

Miller's most famous performance came at the 1973 U.S. Open at Oakmont. He entered the final round trailing by six shots. The course was brutally tough. Only six golfers shot under par in the final round. Miller shot a U.S. Open record 63. He hit all eighteen greens in regulation. The golf writers immediately called it the best ball-striking round ever played at the U.S. Open. That round, it turned out, had an interesting effect on Watson's life.

Miller says that one afternoon in Tucson, he was walking off the golf course after a practice round when he heard a commotion on the 9th green. He walked over and saw a group of caddies shouting and swearing. Then he saw Watson standing over a ball fifteen or twenty feet away from the hole. It took Miller a few minutes to put it all together; Watson was betting them, straight up, that he could make long putt after long putt.

"Who does that?" Miller asked later. "To make money, you have to make more than half of those putts. Who can do that? Who can make more than half of their fifteen- or twenty-footers? That's when I took real notice of Tom Watson. That's when I thought, 'Man, if a guy can putt like that he's going to win some tournaments.'"

Watson's unique ability to make long putts came down to a single word: *conviction*. There are only three ways to miss a putt: you can miss a putt left; you can miss a putt right; or you can leave a putt short. It is possible to hit a putt so hard that it will roll over the hole, but this rarely happens to the world's best golfers.

Watson simply reduced his miss possibilities to two: he hit the ball so hard that he almost never left a putt short. Nobody since the young and daring Arnold Palmer had putted golf balls so hard. There's a reason golfers don't hit their putts that hard; they don't want to roll the ball well past the hole and be faced with a long putt coming back. But Watson's all-consuming conviction was not in the first putt; it was in his complete and unshakable certainty that he would make the comeback putt.

After seeing Watson knock in a four-foot putt without a moment's glance at the break, his Kansas City friend and fellow PGA player Jim Colbert once pointed out, "You might want to take a little bit more time on those short putts."

Watson looked confused. "Why?" he asked.

Watson felt invulnerable on short putts, and that feeling freed him to hit his first putts firmly at the hole. Nobody made more long putts than he did in those days. "He was the coolest player on tour," the future PGA star Davis Love III said. "My dad would say to me, 'Look at how hard he hit that first putt.' He was fearless."

Watson's putting was so good that he kept finding himself in contention; in early 1974 he finished in the top ten in three straight tournaments. Later he finished second at the Byron Nelson Classic, a tournament that would alter his life. But he didn't win any of those tournaments. "I really wasn't a very good player," he recalls. "I wasn't ready to win."

Then he went to Winged Foot Golf Club in Mamaroneck for the 1974 U.S. Open.

Ray Watson raised his son on the U.S. Open. Ray knew every U.S. Open winner going back to an Englishman named Horace Rawlins, who won in Newport, Rhode Island, in 1895. When Tom was young, he and his father would play a little U.S. Open game. Ray would ask, "Who won the U.S. Open in 1910?" Tom was supposed to know not only that Alex Smith won it but that he won it at the St. Martin's Course in Philadelphia. When it came to the U.S. Open, Ray was almost religious in his zeal.

Tom Watson finished twenty-ninth at his first U.S. Open, at Pebble Beach in 1972, and he missed the cut when Miller had his magical final round at Oakmont in 1973. Nobody expected much from him at Winged Foot in 1974. But he turned out to be a central figure in one of the stranger U.S. Opens ever played.

Miller's final round in 1973 had awed golf fans around the world, but it also embarrassed officials at the U.S. Golf

Association, which presents the U.S. Open. The USGA prides itself on creating the most difficult major championship in the world. They do this by mowing tight fairways, growing very high rough, and making sure the greens aren't too soft and receptive. Miller made the U.S. Open look easy in 1973. The next year, the USGA made sure everyone suffered. The tournament would become known as the Massacre at Winged Foot.

Forty-four golfers could not even break 80 on the first day. Nicklaus bogeyed the first four holes and never contended. When someone asked him about the setup at Winged Food, he answered, "Well, the last eighteen holes are pretty tough." Miller was defeated. "This golf course makes you feel like a dog," he said.

After the second day, Palmer was one of four leaders. He talked lovingly about the golf course. "For the first time in a long time, I found myself having to play every kind of shot," he said happily. He then faded. Two-time U.S. Open champion Trevino shot a pair of 78s the first two rounds and missed the cut entirely. "I felt like I was playing miniature golf without sideboards," he grumbled.

When the USGA president Sandy Tatum was asked why the association would set up a golf course that seemed designed to humiliate the world's best players, he offered this famous reply: "We're not trying to embarrass the best players in the world. We're trying to identify them."

Standing out among the wreckage was Tom Watson. Like Palmer, he enjoyed trying to figure out Winged Foot. On the third day he shocked everyone by shooting a 69, 1-under par, and like that he led the U.S. Open by a shot. He found himself in front of a slightly confused national and international media contingent; the only thing any of them knew about Watson was that he had blown the Hawaiian and World Opens. "I think it's because I've been too impatient," he told the reporters. "I've been too eager to win. I've tried to play too fast. I think that's the big thing I've got to try and guard against."

Sportswriters like a clear narrative, and now they had one: Tom Watson versus His Demons. Watson had choked before. Could he overcome his nature and win this U.S. Open on one of the toughest golf courses ever devised for a major championship? Could he hold up under golf's brightest spotlight and win his country's national championship?

No. He could not.

On Sunday, Watson struggled with his game on the front nine, shooting 3-over par, but as he made the turn he was still tied for the lead. There's a famous golf saying: Major championships don't begin until the back nine on Sunday. If that's true, Watson's major championship began on the 10th hole, when he missed the sort of short putt that he never missed. After that, as they say, the wheels fell off. He shot 6-over on the last nine holes and finished five shots behind Hale Irwin.

"Yes, it looks like I blew it," he told reporters. "And you can say I blew it."

He didn't have to worry: the reporters wrote that he blew it.

Here's something wonderful about golf: you can be going along hopelessly, playing the worst round of your life, and then inexplicably you hit an amazing shot that changes everything. That amazing shot, like the sun breaking through the clouds, is why so many people keep playing.

In the Winged Foot clubhouse after the most devastating loss of his young life, Watson felt someone walking toward him, and he looked up to see Byron Nelson. Nelson was sixty-two and still maintained the regal presence of his playing days, when they had called him "Lord Byron." He was a great golfer, once winning eleven tournaments in a row, and he was also one of the game's great gentlemen. For years, the Masters Tournament would pair the final-round leader with Nelson, in homage to Lord Byron and, more, to ease the leader's mind a bit as he faced the extreme pressure. There was no more pleasant a golf partner.

In 1955, for instance, Nelson played the final round with Cary Middlecoff, a gifted and mercurial former dentist who tended to panic when he had the lead. Middlecoff was a beehive of nerves on that Sunday and several times felt like he would fall apart. Then he would hear the gentle Texas twang of Nelson: "Come on, Doc. Play golf. You're okay." Middlecoff went on to win easily.

Now Nelson brought a Coke to Watson and asked if he could sit down. Nelson had been one of the television broadcasters for the tournament, and he had closely watched Watson's collapse. He said, "Tom, I'm sorry you had such a bad day. I've seen quite a few people who've been in the lead but not played good the final round until they had a few tries at it." Watson nodded as if he understood, but he was despondent. He was three years into his career, and he had not won a tournament. He had been in position to win what his father considered the most important tournament, and he had faltered.

"Look," Nelson said, "I'm not working with anyone right now. If any time you'd like to work with me, I give you permission to call me." Nelson stopped there for emphasis. "No one else has that privilege."

Then he said, "I think you are going to be a great player."

Two weeks later, Tom Watson shot a 69—the lowest round of the day—and overcame a six-shot deficit to win his first tournament, the Western Open at Butler National Golf Club in Oak

OVERESTIMATE THE WIND

Tom was a great, great wind player. Sometimes it felt to me like
he could hear the wind talking.

GARY PLAYER, NINE-TIME MAJOR CHAMPION

Watson does not like playing golf on sunny days. The sort of sunny,
windless golf that people in dark offices dream about day after day
bores him the way highway driving might bore a race car driver
or a game of Monopoly might bore a real estate magnate. Watson
needs wind in his golf. "If I look outside and see the sun out and
the trees still," he says, "I would rather do something else but golf."

Add wind, though, and Watson lights up like a child with a
kite. The wind makes every hole different from the way it was the
day before. The wind devises puzzles to solve. Watson relied on
his caddie, Bruce Edwards, for yardage and occasional putting
thoughts and emotional support, but he never asked Edwards to
read the wind. That was his job. "Come on, man," he implores
when thinking of golfers who ask their caddies where the wind is
coming from, "you've got to *feel* the shot."

Watson says he did not always get such enjoyment when playing in the wind. He hit his shots very high as a young man, and he

would watch the wind knock some of his best shots out of the sky. But he adapted. The first step, he says, was learning to enjoy the challenge of playing in the wind. He thinks amateur golfers often defeat themselves with a negative attitude on windy days.

The second step he sums up in three words: Overestimate the wind. "It never ceases to amaze me that even good players, when hitting into the wind, will come up well short. This is even when they hit a good shot. It's because they don't overestimate the force of the wind in their face.

"I will play a two-, three-, four-club wind sometimes. Stan [Thirsk] made it very clear playing in the wind when I was a kid. Stan said if you swing easier at the ball, you put less spin on it. Therefore the ball will penetrate through the air a little bit better without rising up in the air. That means taking more club."

Overestimate the wind. Watson says this is something larger than golf. Anticipate a bigger problem. Prepare for an unforeseen hurdle. Expect things to get complicated. Expect traffic to be worse than usual. Presume that repairs will cost more than the estimate. Overestimate the wind.

"Won't overestimating the wind sometimes backfire?" I ask him. "Won't you sometimes play too much wind and hit a bad shot because of that?"

"Let me ask you," he responds: "How many times do you see a golfer hit the ball over the green into a stiff wind? Not very often. That's the reason it works. When you overestimate the wind, you're not really overestimating. You're just seeing things more clearly."

HOLE NO. 6

From the time he was in junior high school, Jack Nicklaus had reigned supreme in Tom Watson's mind. Nicklaus had vanquished his hero, Arnold Palmer. Nicklaus had pushed the boundaries of golf excellence. When Watson first came on the PGA Tour, Nicklaus was a faraway star playing what seemed a different game. Watson would watch him, follow him, study him. One weekend in New Orleans, he walked with the gallery after Nicklaus. "It was hard with the fans out there, and I'm trying to see what club he's hitting off the thirteenth tee or where he's laying up or what type of shot he's playing. But I studied him every chance I could."

At the beginning of 1975, though, Watson felt ready to challenge Nicklaus. He had won a tournament. He had contended at the U.S. Open. Golfers and fans began to talk about him more and more; someone coined the phrase *Watson par*. A Watson par might go like this: Watson would hit a terrible drive into the woods somewhere. He often hit terrible drives then. He would smile his hard smile, find the ball behind a tree or barely visible in high grass, and hit a deft rescue shot to the fairway somewhere.

He would hit a good third shot that might stop eight or ten feet from the hole. And then he would make the putt for a par.

Watson made Watson pars so often and with such astonishing shots and putts that a little bit of a legend built up around him. There seemed no trouble he could not overcome.

"I never saw anybody—*anybody*—who was as positive after a bad shot as Tom Watson," Johnny Miller said. "It was crazy, really. He just never let it bother him."

In Augusta at the Masters, Watson got his chance to match up with Nicklaus. Tom Weiskopf, one of the fleet of "next Nicklaus" golfers who came onto the Tour, led the Masters going into Sunday. Nicklaus was a shot back; Miller was four back; Watson five. The Masters in those days mixed and matched the Sunday pairings. For some reason that neither golfer remembers, that day Watson and Nicklaus were paired, and Weiskopf and Miller played in the ground behind them. It made for great television.

Watson wasn't a big part of the story. He played reasonably well, but Nicklaus, Weiskopf, and Miller left him behind. The CBS producer Frank Chirkinian gleefully described how the day unfolded like a perfectly structured drama. Nicklaus was the reigning king. Weiskopf was the dark and grim younger brother who longed for his moment. Miller was the blond and heroic prince making his charge. The crescendo came when Nicklaus teed off on the 16th hole. "Get up!" he shouted at the ball; he had hit a poor shot. The ball did not get up. It settled forty treacherous feet away from the cup; he would need all of his skill and nerve just to two-putt the hole.

Meanwhile, back on the 15th hole, Weiskopf and Miller were in position to make eagles or birdies and take the tournament away from Nicklaus.

After Nicklaus hit his shot, Watson played his role in the

theater, plunking his tee shot in the water. He walked all the way to the green to see if his ball had crossed land; it had not. So he walked back to the tee, hit the ball again, and again hit into the water. Finally, on his third attempt, he put the ball on dry land.

Chirkinian could not believe his telecasting fortune. He did not know anything about Watson yet, but he did know that Watson's fumbling had given Weiskopf and Miller time to hit their approach shots. This set up a remarkable television scene. The 15th green and 16th tee are only a few yards away from each other. Nicklaus would see exactly what Weiskopf and Miller did, and they would watch Nicklaus's putt. Chirkinian built the drama by directing his camera to first show Weiskopf, then Nicklaus, then Miller. For Chirkinian it felt like the moment before a heavyweight boxing fight. Weiskopf putted first. He made his ten-foot putt to take the lead, and Chirkinian turned the camera on Nicklaus. "And that," Ben Wright announced, "is going to be evil music ringing in Nicklaus's ears."

Then it was Nicklaus's turn. He faced what seemed to the broadcasters and gallery to be an impossible putt. But he had decided he could make it. As golf fans watched, Nicklaus slammed the putt up the hill. When the ball was ten feet from the hole, his caddy Willie Peter lifted his arm in triumph. The ball dropped in the hole, and the normally stoic Nicklaus leaped in the air and ran a few steps around the green. The CBS announcer Henry Longhurst countered Ben Wright's poetry by saying, "Did you ever see one like that? I think that's one of the greatest putts I've ever seen in my life. And now Weiskopf will have to take it as he dished it out before."

Nicklaus won the Masters. And Watson watched this one differently, not so much as an admirer but as a competitor. He was beginning to understand just how high he had to climb.

. . .

Two months later, at the 1975 U.S. Open in Medinah Country Club in Illinois, Watson started off remarkably well. He built a three-shot lead after two rounds and tied the thirty-six-hole U.S. Open scoring record. He was playing exuberant golf. He told reporters he had left the year-old disappointment of Winged Foot behind him: "The pressure might be a little bit less than last year [at] Winged Foot. I feel more sure."

Then Saturday came, and Watson almost four-putted the first hole; he just about whiffed on a three-foot putt. He was visibly shaken. He bogeyed three of the first four holes. Something about his inability to hold up under the intensity brought out the worst in a few golf fans. "Remember Winged Foot!" they shouted. Watson was affected. He shot 78 and fell three shots off the lead.

"It rips me up inside," he said, "but Sunday is another day. I can still win."

But Sunday was very much like Saturday. His touch had left him. He shot 76 and once again left the stage to Nicklaus. The Golden Bear had not played well all week, but one of the things Nicklaus had come to understand was that he did not need to play well in order to win major championships. He needed only to play smarter than everyone else. With three holes to go, he found himself near the lead, and he knew precisely what was left for him to do.

"Par, par, par wins this tournament," he said to himself. This was Nicklaus's internal clock at work. He sensed that even though he still trailed, he needed only to stay steady to the end. The other golfers, he knew, would come back to him. And he was right, except he didn't make three pars coming in. He made three bogeys instead and lost by two shots. The collapse was shocking to him. "I gave away the tournament," he moaned afterward.

Still, Nicklaus had fifteen major championships, more than anyone else, and he could afford to lose one every now and again. (And he did lose more than his share, finishing second a record nineteen times.) The Medinah U.S. Open was much harder on Watson, who had just let another chance slip away. He was playing the best golf of his life. He had proven—to Linda, to his father, to himself—that he was good enough to make a living at this game. But somewhere along the way the goal had changed. He no longer wanted just to make a living. He wanted to beat Jack Nicklaus.

Everything about Carnoustie Golf Links on the east coast of Scotland is historic and gothic and frightening. For a golfer, it seems set in a Charles Dickens novel. Locals say they have been playing golf at Carnoustie—or *gawf,* as it is written in the Parish Records of 1560—for four hundred years. When the wind howls and the rain blows sideways, golfers today have no more chance of holding their own than they did all those years ago.

Carnoustie is one of the toughest golf courses in Great Britain, which makes it one of the toughest courses in the world. Before the 1975 Open, only five golfers had ever shot better than 70 at a Carnoustie Open Championship. The most famous of those was Ben Hogan's final-round 68 to clinch the 1953 Open; that was the only Open Championship Hogan ever entered. His play on that final day was so inspired that afterward the 6th hole was renamed "Hogan's Alley." Fifteen years later Gary Player won the Open at Carnoustie without breaking 70 once.

This seemed the unlikeliest place for Watson to compete. He had never played the Open before, and he almost immediately did not like the golf course. Plus, just before heading to Carnoustie, he had to ask his first agent, Hughes Norton, to find him a caddie. His now-trusted American caddie, Bruce Edwards, had run into visa problems (he didn't have one) and motivational problems (the trip cost a lot of money). Norton found a hard-drinking, chain-smoking English character named Alfie Fyles who had caddied for Gary Player when he won at Carnoustie. "He knows the course as well as anybody," Norton said. Watson was satisfied until he went out with Fyles to the fierce 1st hole. "Hit it there," Fyles said, and Watson complied, hitting a shot he felt was just about perfect. But when they walked out to the spot, the ball was nowhere to be found. The two looked around for a while, until finally and reluctantly they looked in a pot bunker forty yards away. There was Watson's ball. It was like an anti-magic trick.

"This isn't golf," Watson muttered to himself. "This is luck."

No, he didn't like Carnoustie. He didn't like his caddie, at least at first. He didn't like links golf. And yet he played inspired golf in the first round. He shot a 71, which normally would have put him in the lead. But the wind, which always roared at Carnoustie, was positively still. There was no rain. Carnoustie was unexpectedly naked. Seven golfers broke 70 on the first day. One of them was Nicklaus, who was still steaming about giving away the U.S. Open.

On the second day, eight more golfers broke 70. A South African named Bobby Cole, who had never finished in the top ten at a major championship, set the course record with a 66. Then, with the wind still down, Cole shot another 66 the next day, but he no longer held the record. A fun-loving Australian named Jack Newton shot a 65.

The golfers were embarrassing the venerable old course, and Watson joined in. He shot 67 and 69 in the second and third rounds to put himself in fourth place, just three shots behind

Cole, the leader. He was still uncomfortable with the mysteries of links golf, but he was beginning what would be a lifelong love affair with Scotland and its people.

In those days the Open always ended on Saturday, and the Saturday morning before his final round he heard a knock on the door of his small house in Monifieth, a town about five miles west of Carnoustie. Watson opened the door to a little girl, who gave him something in foil. "This is for good luck," she said. Inside the foil was a sprig of white heather.

There's a Celtic folktale of a beautiful woman named Malvina who was to be married to the great warrior Oscar. But Oscar was mortally wounded in battle; in his final moments he picked a sprig of purple heather and had a messenger take it to Malvina. When she was told that Oscar had died, she began to cry, and her tears turned the heather white. Malvina's prayer was this: "May the White Heather, symbol of my sorrow, bring good fortune to all who find it."

Watson did not know the story, but he thanked the girl and put the white heather into his golf bag. Then he headed to the golf course, not knowing he was carrying Malvina's prayer.

What is good fortune? Is it a bolt of luck that hits you unexpectedly? Or is it something else? When Watson got to the golf course that Saturday, he ran into Byron Nelson, who was broadcasting the tournament. Nelson and Watson had grown closer since their encounter at the U.S. Open; Watson had won the Byron Nelson Classic seven weeks earlier, much to Nelson's delight. Still, Nelson had always seemed reluctant to give Watson advice. He tended instead simply to encourage Watson to trust himself.

That day, though, Nelson had something specific in mind. The wind had picked up at Carnoustie. The golf course would bare its teeth on this day, and Nelson knew that most of the other golfers would not be ready for it.

"Tom, I've avoided giving you specific advice," Nelson began, "but I'm going to give you some advice today. You are always very good about leaving behind bad shots and looking forward. But today you need to be better at that than you've ever been in your life. You're going to make mistakes. Everyone is. The wind is up—those last four holes are going to be really hard. You're playing the best golf of anyone here. Remember those last four holes."

Nelson's words had a dramatic effect on Watson. He relaxed. It was as if, all at once, he realized that he could win without being perfect.

The 18th hole at Carnoustie is the site of the most disastrous collapse in golf history. The collapse happened long after Watson stepped to the tee that Saturday in 1975. The protagonist was a likable Frenchman named Jean van de Velde who had never come close to winning anything of note until he came to Carnoustie for the 1999 Open Championship. Van de Velde was something of a character. He wore a Disney logo on his shirt because he was the golf pro at Disneyland in Paris. "I test all the rides," he told reporters that week, "and walk around with all the characters."

That year the wind howled and rain fell and golfers succumbed to Carnoustie's will. Tiger Woods finished 10-over par. Watson, who was forty-nine and had come to Carnoustie hoping he could recapture some old magic, shot 13-over on just the first two days. All of the world's great golfers coughed and wheezed, and only this self-effacing character from France with Mickey Mouse near his heart seemed immune to Carnoustie's supremacy. After three rounds, he led by five shots. As he stepped up to the 18th and final hole, he led by three shots. He needed only a double bogey to win. His victory was assured.

Only it wasn't. The 18th hole at Carnoustie is a chilling hole, as intimidating as any in Great Britain, and van de Velde hit his driver way to the right into the rough. While the television announcers wondered why he had used a driver, the riskiest of clubs, he found his ball and was surprised to see that he had a clean lie. He decided to hit his second shot toward the green rather than simply punching the ball back into the fairway. His second shot flew into a grandstand and bounced back into deep rough. "His golfing brain stopped about ten minutes ago," a BBC announcer said.

Van de Velde tried to chip his third shot out of the rough and onto the green, and he hit it into a creek instead. He took off his shoes and rolled up his pants and went into the water after his ball. "Well, you get your money's worth from the French," one thoroughly amused BBC announcer said. Just as van de Velde stepped into the creek, the ball submerged and disappeared. In the press conference afterward, he re-created this scene, in which he could actually hear the golf ball talking to him. "Bye-bye," the ball said. "No Open Championship for you."

His fifth shot went into a bunker. His sixth shot—the last one that could have still won him the Open—rolled five feet from the cup. Van de Velde ended his nightmare in a three-man playoff, which he promptly lost. This is the horror of the 18th hole at Carnoustie. And this is where the young Tom Watson found his voice.

Watson approached the 18th hole on that final round in 1975 fully aware that he needed a birdie to give himself a chance. He was 8-under par, three shots behind the leader, Jack Newton, and two shots behind Newton's pursuer, Bobby Cole. Watson had watched Nicklaus enough to know that the way to win major championships was not to go chasing low scores but to wait for pressure to take its toll on everyone else. Nine under, Watson decided, would be good enough to give him a real shot.

Nicklaus had already made the same projection. He was 8-under par as he went into the last four holes, and he turned to his caddie, Angelo Argea, and said, "One birdie will take it, Angie. Those guys are going to fly apart back there." Nicklaus couldn't get that one birdie—instead he made four straight pars—but, as always, his internal clock was synchronized to the moment.

Johnny Miller's internal clock was not; this was perhaps the difference between Nicklaus and Miller. He came to the last four holes at 10-under par, in perfect position to win. But he looked back at the leaderboard of top scores and decided he needed one more birdie. He played too aggressively and made two bogeys instead, playing himself out of a chance.

Watson had played well all day. His putting touch abandoned him for a time—he three-putted three greens in a row—but otherwise he played with the patience and positive energy that Nelson had recommended. Watson had a superb chance for birdie on the 17th hole but missed the putt, so he came to the 18th believing that a birdie would at least get him into a playoff. This was the scenario he had imagined a million times in his life: one hole, one birdie, a major championship on the line. He striped a drive down the middle and hit his 9-iron to twenty feet from the flag. He then rammed home the birdie putt. He had gotten his 9-under. Now he just needed to see if the leaders really would fly apart, as Nelson and Nicklaus had predicted.

They did. Cole bogeyed 15, 16, and 17. Newton bogeyed the same three holes but held it together enough to make par on the

18th, to force an eighteen-hole playoff with Watson for the Open Championship. They were two young men, almost exactly the same age, each attempting to win a major championship for the first time. But they were not otherwise alike. When asked how he planned to prepare, Watson talked about his mental approach to dealing with pressure. Newton, when asked the same question, smiled slyly and said, "Get drunk again."

The playoff too came down to the 18th. Watson and Newton were tied. When Newton hit his second shot into a bunker, Watson aimed for the heart of the green. He took two putts and won his first major championship. Many of the stories that followed talked about how Watson had slain the choker inside.

SCORE WELL WHEN NOT PLAYING WELL

There are only five tournaments in my life where going in I thought I was going to win. . . . I won a lot more when I wasn't playing well than when I was.

TOM WATSON

I have won eighteen majors and I can promise you that I didn't play well in at least a dozen of them.

JACK NICKLAUS

Byron Nelson often told Watson a story about a day at Augusta when his beautiful swing misfired. He could not hit the ball into the fairway, and he could not get the ball on the green. He felt out of control, a rare feeling for Lord Byron. He managed a par 72 and walked off the final green muttering.

After the match, he complained to his friend Eddie Lowery, who had gained his own golfing fame as the ten-year-old caddie for Francis Ouimet at his upset victory in the 1913 U.S. Open.

"Eddie," Nelson said, "I believe that was as poorly as I can remember playing."

"On the contrary, Byron," Lowery said. "This was the finest round of golf you have ever played."

Nelson eyed Lowery coolly.

"Because," Lowery continued, "you played that badly and you *still* shot a seventy-two."

For Watson, that story offers the secret of competitive golf. He hears from weekend golfers all the time who talk about how they didn't drive the ball well, didn't hit their irons well, didn't putt well, and so on. They see this as the reason they shot high scores. Only Watson doesn't see it that way. "That's a normal state of the game, even for the best players," he says. "That's golf."

Watson says the days when he or Nicklaus or Tiger Woods play really well—when they feel in control of every aspect of their game—are rare. Playing well is not something even professional golfers can count on. "Winning golf does not come down to playing better than everyone else. It comes down to thinking better than everyone else."

Funny thing is, Nicklaus says exactly the same thing: "I have always felt that the mettle of a player is not how well he plays when he's playing well, but how well he scores and plays when he's playing poorly."

So what are the keys to scoring well when you're not playing well? These are the things Watson stresses all the time: forget about bad shots, don't try for the hero shot, aim for the spots with the least trouble, take one shot of medicine here to save two or three strokes later. "If there's a tough bunker on the right of the green, and you're not confident in your bunker play, aim for the left side. Or take one club less and leave the ball short. Play the shot that keeps you out of that bunker. Think a shot ahead. Think about what you *are* doing well and try to play to your strength that day."

"So what happens," I ask, "when you're not doing anything well?"

Watson smiles. "It happens," he says. "And those are rough days. But those are the days that define you. Like Eddie Lowery told Byron, those are the days when you can play your finest rounds."

HOLE NO. 7

Before the 1976 golf season, many people wrote that Watson had arrived as a blossoming young superstar. That's how quickly a sports narrative changes. Months earlier he was widely viewed as a choker who might never win anything of consequence. Then he won the Open Championship and instantly became a brilliant young golfer who could challenge Nicklaus. Watson would come to resent the black-and-white extremes of the golf press. But he was just twenty-six then and more befuddled by the new narrative than anything else.

Watson did not feel any different. He was proud of his Open Championship win, of course, and he believed he had earned it. But he still thought his game wasn't good enough. "At that point," he said later, "I wanted to be the best golfer in the world."

To become the best golfer in the world, he needed to hit the ball more consistently. It was that simple. He had won tournaments and a lot of money and a major championship on audacity and verve and great putting. It was a lot like the Palmer plan. But Watson knew the limits of that game against Nicklaus. He needed to control his ball flight, and to do that he did what came naturally to him: he practiced obsessively. His caddie Bruce Edwards would say that Watson practiced more after the Open Championship than before: "He was harder on himself than ever before, I think. It seemed like just when everybody was finally beginning to realize just how good Tom was, he was thinking how much he still needed to improve. . . . He always had so much drive. People never understood how big his dream was."

Watson's problem was a hook. On occasion, he would hit a nasty little right-to-left hook that would put him in deep trouble. But the larger problem was that he usually did this when a tournament was on the line. Early in 1976, he led the Los Angeles Open by three shots heading into the final round. He led Hale Irwin by five shots after only three holes. The hook showed up uninvited. He missed a green. He hit it under a tree. He missed a fairway.

And once Watson started hitting hooks, other parts of his game disintegrated. He missed a short putt, then another one. When Irwin took the lead, Watson knew he needed to hit a good drive. Instead he hooked another one into the rough. Irwin won by two shots. Watson had played great golf all week—even finishing second, he had broken the tournament record—but when it came down to winning and losing, Irwin's swing held up under the strain. Watson's did not.

"Damn it," he told himself, "I'm not good enough yet."

It is one of golf's age-old questions: How do you stop a hook? Hogan often said it was his effort to stop hooking the ball that led to the Secret. The same question besieged Watson in 1976. Edwards would stand behind him and watch him practice hour after hour, day after day. He hoped only to hear three words. When Watson figured out something on the practice range, he would turn to Edwards, smile a little, and say, "I got it."

"When he said that," Edwards explained, "it was off to the races."

But Watson could not find what he was looking for. He went to Augusta with every intention of contending again; instead he shot a 77 on the first day and played himself right out of the tournament. He went to defend his title at the Byron Nelson Classic and even under the watchful eye of his mentor barely made the cut and finished forty-fourth.

In Memphis two weeks later, he hurt his wrist, which forced him to miss the first Memorial Tournament, Nicklaus's tournament. The Memorial had been in Nicklaus's mind for a long time. His father's hero, Bobby Jones, had been the golfer of his age, but his lasting contribution to golf was building the Augusta National Golf Club and then inviting a bunch of his friends to a tournament he called the Masters. Nicklaus wanted the Memorial to be an homage to Jones—and, even more, to Charlie Nicklaus.

"Of course I'd like to win," Nicklaus said before the first Memorial. "But this time, in this tournament, I really have mixed emotions about it. It may look better if someone else won."

Watson would have loved to be that someone else, but instead he was home recovering and practicing his swing in front of a mirror. Roger Maltbie took the championship. Watson did not return until the U.S. Open, where he finished seven shots back. That was really the story of Watson's year. For the most part, he played okay. He missed only three cuts all year and regularly finished in the top ten. His friends saw nothing at all wrong with his game; he was contending, he was making money, he was a major championship winner. Even Nelson told Watson to ease up on himself.

But Watson could not ease up. Though he was widely acknowledged as one of the world's great putters, he asked the putting guru Jerry Barber for help. He kept returning to Nelson for more practical advice. To placate his apprentice, Lord Byron told him to slow down and not to waggle the club so violently before his shots. But he kept insisting that Watson did not need to change anything. "You've got a great swing, Tom," he said. "You just have to have faith in it."

After Watson won the 1975 British Open, he met with his caddie Alfie Fyles to settle the week's finances. Fyles was a professional caddie in the fullest sense of the word; he believed deeply that it was a caddie's responsibility to lead his player to victory, and he believed just as strongly that it was the winning player's responsibility to tip generously.

In a classic *Sports Illustrated* story, Frank Deford wrote about the exchange that followed. Fyles was a proper British caddie. He did not step off distances for any man; he eyed the distance. He drank and scrapped in the bars. Watson would always remember the time Fyles showed up at the golf course with a beauty of a black eye. "I had a bit of an altercation last night," Fyles explained.

"Was it over me?" Watson asked.

"It happened to be, Mister," Fyles said. (He always called Watson "Mister.")

"Who won?"

"Who do you think, sir?"

Fyles often talked in Cockney slang, using rhyming words. "Apples and pears," for instance, meant "stairs." When Fyles said, "Say it à la mode," he meant "Say it in code." "Get the dog and bone" meant "Answer the phone." "Trouble and strife," of course, meant "the wife." That evening after Watson won the Open, the Cockney slang that most concerned Fyles was "the Gregory Peck," which meant "the check." He had guided a greenhorn American playing on his first links course to the Open Championship. And when Watson gave him the Gregory Peck, Fyles couldn't Adam and Eve it (believe it).

"You must need this more than I do," Fyles shouted, and he threw the Gregory Peck on the floor. Linda Watson, who handled all the finances, began to speak, but Fyles made it clear that he didn't want to work for old trouble and strife. This got Watson's temper going, and Fyles picked up his Gregory Peck and stormed out ("Before Tom could take me seriously").

That meant when Watson went to Royal Birkdale to defend his Open Championship in 1976, he was without Alfie Fyles. Instead he brought along Edwards, who was still smarting over missing his friend's 1975 victory. It was an exciting time for both of them. Then the tournament began. Watson triple-bogeyed the first hole basically to end his defense. He did not survive the cut, and before he left he suffered one final indignity. On his last day, Watson was playing terribly, and on the 10th hole, while trying to get out of a bunker, he cut the golf ball with a swing. He gave the ball to Edwards and put a new ball in play.

Watson came to the end needing a decent final hole just to stay in the tournament. He promptly hit his ball out of bounds. Edwards, who was up the fairway waiting, had to race back and get him a golf ball to use. He ran as fast as he could, mindlessly picked out a ball, and threw it on one hop to Watson. Years later, when Edwards was dying of ALS, he talked to the author John Feinstein about how proud he was of that throw.

Trouble was, he had thrown the ball Watson had taken out of play earlier. By the rules of golf, playing a ball you already took out of play is a two-stroke penalty. Watson missed the cut by one shot.

Edwards was mortified, but Watson took it in stride. "It was an honest mistake and it could happen to anyone," he said. "And it didn't matter anyway." He was fifteen shots behind the leader, Johnny Miller, and had no chance to win. The next year, though, he rehired Fyles for the British Open.

Golf takes illogical turns. A serious golfer goes to the practice range day after day looking for answers. He tries to keep his head straighter. He tucks in his right elbow. He widens his stance. He narrows his stance. He shortens his swing or lengthens it. He fumbles around with the takeaway, tries various maneuvers at the top of the swing, reconsiders his follow-through. A golfer is a tinkerer. For the longest time, nothing good happens. The hook keeps hooking. The putts keep drifting off. The sense of control never quite locks in.

One day, the golfer finds himself in Japan, playing in a pro-am, and he's playing lousy and feeling lousy. His ball is on a slope, well below his feet. It's just one shot, one of millions he will hit in his lifetime. Only it isn't. Watson hit this shot, and everything changed.

"I made an adjustment on the takeaway that kept the club face looking at the ball a bit longer," he says almost forty years later, and even though the words are technical golf talk, the look on his face is still wide-eyed with discovery. "I kept the face looking down the line a bit more rather than rotating, and I hit a very solid shot for basically the first time [that] day. I went right to the practice tee and hit a few shots, and I thought, 'I got it.'"

"One shot?" I ask him.

"One shot."

He promptly won that tournament in Japan—setting a course record along the way—and everything changed. Golf makes no sense. One day Watson suspected that he would never get it, never find the key that opened up his game. Then he hit the shot. "And life's good. Everything changed. Even the food tastes better."

The golf world would quickly find out what "I got it" meant. In the third tournament of 1977, at Pebble Beach, Watson played masterfully. He hit every green in regulation on Saturday. On Sunday he played great again and almost made a hole-in-one on the 17th hole. He broke the Bing Crosby National Pro-Am Tournament record by four shots.

A week later he set the tournament record at the Andy Williams San Diego Open and won by five shots. Dom Mirandi, the official scorer of the PGA Tour, told the Associated Press, "Well, it looks like we have another Nicklaus on our hands."

The writers, so eager to call him the next Nicklaus a year earlier, didn't buy it this time. A few weeks later, when Watson took the lead into the final day at the Tournament Players Championship, the press was notably skeptical. *Let's see how he handles Sunday* was the theme.

Watson was dreadful on Sunday. He held a two-shot lead for much of the day and then lost his game. He shot 41 on the back nine to lose by four shots. The winner, Mark Hayes, thought Watson simply had problems with the wind ("He hits the ball so high," Hayes said), but the old choking theme was whispered again.

"He knows he blew it," his wife told reporters. "But he hasn't let it bother him. Oh, I guess it bothers him, but he doesn't dwell on it. He's put it out of his mind."

A week later, in Hilton Head, South Carolina, the reporters' hunch that Watson was again choking seemed confirmed. On the first three days, he played much better than anyone; he took a four-shot lead into Sunday. But again he lost, this time in spectacular, disastrous fashion. On the 14th hole, clinging to a two-shot lead, he hit one of the worst shots of his professional life: an iron shot that barely seemed to get into the air and then dropped helplessly into the water. Watson, who prided himself on keeping his emotions locked inside, noticeably dropped his head. That led to a double bogey. And that led to one more loss.

"He didn't say anything," his playing partner Ben Crenshaw said. "What could he say?"

The Masters was one week away, and the narrative was clear: Tom Watson still did not know how to win.

A POSITIVE THOUGHT

Sometimes you play a shot that you are uncomfortable with. That's okay. You know the negatives of the shot. You know the parameters of the bunkers, the water hazards, the out-of-bounds placement. It's all right to be negative about it. But the last thought you have before you swing the club—that better be a positive swing thought.

TOM WATSON

Watson is among many who believe that visualizing a shot is one of the most important parts of playing good golf. But for most of us, it's a hard thing to do. For one thing, we don't have Watson's imagination. For another, the shot we hit often bears no resemblance at all to the shot we saw in our minds. After visualizing a high cut that dances around the cup and then hitting a low screamer that plugs into a bunker, how can you help but wonder, What's the point?

The point, Watson says, is that positive energy fuels the golf swing. No golfer needs to be told that many more bad things than good things can happen when you hit a golf ball. Golf's a hard game. At the same time, thinking about how hard a game golf is has never helped anyone play the game better, just as thinking about the intimidating length of a marathon will not help anyone get to the finish line.

One of the things Watson takes great pride in is that, with rare exceptions, he did not think negative thoughts when hitting the ball. He walked fast and he played fast, and that was because he had no interest in lingering on the challenges or the potential calamities. He got to the ball, looked at his lie, gauged the wind, considered the shot he wanted to hit and the trouble he wanted to avoid, and then he stepped up, visualized the shot, believed in what he had envisioned, and hit the ball. That was all.

"Were you a scoreboard watcher?" I ask him.

"Oh yeah. Absolutely. I always wanted to know exactly where I stood."

So I ask him how he put the situation out of his mind as he prepared for his next shot.

"I didn't put it out of my mind. It was there, just like everything else. When I talk about positive swing thoughts . . . not everything is positive. Sometimes you're facing a really hard shot where the negatives are a lot bigger than the positives. Sometimes someone is charging and your lead is dwindling. There are always negatives in the game of golf, and you can't play this game without having those thoughts.

"But once you've weighed all of them, that's when you need to clearly see the shot you want to hit and have enough belief in yourself that you will hit the shot. I see golfers hit a poor shot, and I'll say to them, 'What were you thinking before you hit the shot?' More often than not, they weren't thinking anything. They just hit and hope. It's hard to hit good shots that way."

I ask Watson if he himself ever had trouble visualizing shots.

"Sure I did. Some days are better than others. Some days you see everything in full focus, and other days you don't. But golf is like that. Sometimes you can do everything right, visualize the shot, be positive and then hit a terrible shot. And sometimes you do everything wrong, and you get lucky. But you wouldn't want to count on that."

HOLE NO. 8

Herbert Warren Wind wrote sweetly about golf for *Sports Illustrated* and *The New Yorker* for many years. He was the most respected golf writer in America. Wind was a reserved man, always impeccably dressed in tweed, and he spoke with a slight British accent he might have picked up while studying at Cambridge.

Wind was, first, a poet. His first piece in *The New Yorker* was a poem titled "Upbringing." It is a lyrical little piece about sons and how they count. The elevator operator's son counts by ones, of course, and the porter's son counts by fives. And then he got to the golfer's son.

The golfer's son counts:
1, 2, 3, fore, 5, 6, 7. And balks
At counting any higher.

When Wind began to write about golf, he brought with him the poet's soul. While walking the 11th, 12th, and 13th, that beautiful bend of holes, at Augusta National he thought of an old jazz record and named the holes "the Amen Corner." He pronounced it "Ah-men," rhyming with Brahmin.

Wind wore his feelings about golf openly—"He really gave you a heaping measure of his love of the game," the writer John Updike said—and he believed more than anything that it should be a gentleman's game. Because of this, he never quite got over the way Watson was treated by the press at the 1977 Masters. In a profile of Watson for *The New Yorker* he wrote:

> I cannot remember another athlete being subjected in recent times to anything like the treatment that Watson had to put up with when he arrived at the Augusta National. Most media people are sensitive enough to know what to say and what not to say to someone who has just been through a painful experience, but at every press conference with Watson that I attended before the start of the tournament there were always a few people who had to ask in so many words, "Why do you think you choked at Sawgrass and Harbour Town?"
>
> I don't know how Watson found the supernal restraint to answer these questions politely and reasonably, but he did.

Watson says he found the restraint because he had already asked himself all the same questions. He concluded that he did not choke, not in the way that the sportswriters meant it. They thought of choking as a human frailty, like a lack of courage or a lack of competitive fire. Watson knew he did not lack either. He was a competitor. He was Ray Watson's son.

Watson believed he lost because his swing was not sound enough; it broke down in big moments. When he had control of his swing, he played well. When he did not have control, he choked. It was that simple to him. "I didn't believe in my swing," he told *The New York Times* upon arriving in Augusta. "I think that's different than choking. . . . Everybody chokes. I choke. But when I'm swinging well I don't tend to choke as much as when I'm swinging badly."

He felt he was swinging well. He had played better golf than anyone for the first three months of the year. The collapses at the Players Championship and Hilton Head were just a few remnants of his old habits. But there at Augusta, while talking with Byron Nelson, he felt ready to put away those old habits. When the questions about choking were hurled at him, he smiled a grim smile and answered politely. Deep inside he thought, "This is the week all that choking talk ends forever."

Hart Schaffner & Marx, one of America's biggest manufacturers of menswear, declared Masters week 1977 "Jack Nicklaus Week." In stores all over the country, Jack Nicklaus suits were on sale for less than $200. Blazers and sports coats were selling for as low as $145. Slacks were $39.50.

"Five-time Masters winner Jack Nicklaus knows championship quality," began an advertisement for Hamilton's ("Fine clothing for gentlemen and their sons, since 1873") in Traverse City, Michigan.

"Perfection is a lifestyle with five-time Masters winner Jack Nicklaus," was the ad for Komito's in downtown Mansfield, Ohio.

"A champion knows performance when he sees it," was the pitch from Bledsoe's ("Where Quality Is a Tradition") of Flagstaff, Arizona.

Nicklaus was often called a legend. This annoyed him. "Legend" suggests the past tense. He did not see himself in the past tense. He went into the 1977 season with the intention of fulfilling his greatest ambition: the Grand Slam. That meant winning all four major championships in one calendar year. It was the one golf achievement that had eluded him. "I cannot achieve what I want in golf without winning the Masters," he said leading into the tournament. "It is the first."

Nicklaus was throwing down the challenge. He skipped a tournament to come to Augusta early to prepare. He had heard again and again about the young golfers who had played well in the first three months: Bruce Lietzke, Gary Koch, Mark Hayes, and, of course, Watson. "Early in the year, you usually have some new players winning tournaments," he said in a tone that the press found dismissive. "There's just more of them this time."

Watson, as many expected, was the best player at the Masters for the first two days. He was tied for the lead on Friday, though he would have held the lead alone had he not hooked his 5-iron on the 18th hole (that damned hook!) and bogeyed. The *New York Times* columnist Dave Anderson overheard someone in the crowd grumble, "Tom Watson even finds a way to blow a thirty-six-hole lead."

The press conference after that was basically a repeat of the press conferences he'd had all week, only louder. Again and again he answered questions about his choking past politely and directly. Bruce Edwards had a favorite story about Watson. Once, at a tournament at Pebble Beach, Watson hit a wild shot that flew out of bounds and into the sea. Edwards noticed that Watson watched the ball long after he knew its watery destination. And he kept staring long after the ball had disappeared.

"Why did you keep watching that ball?" Edwards had asked.

"Because that's my punishment," Watson replied.

Perhaps Watson saw the many questions about choking as his punishment for blowing the Tournament Players Championship and the Heritage Classic in Hilton Head and, going back, blowing the U.S. Open when he was younger. On Saturday he shot a 70 and shared the lead with another bright young golfer, Ben Crenshaw. Again Watson faced all the same questions about choking. Again he answered them directly.

Nicklaus meanwhile was three shots back and feeling pretty good. He had nice things to say about Crenshaw. "He plays a little bit like I do," Nicklaus told reporters. "He overpowers a lot of golf courses. He should win this tournament several times."

He did not say anything about Watson.

Years later Nicklaus would admit that he had not figured out Watson. Two years earlier he had seen Watson fall apart at the Masters when the pressure thickened. He would assume, until shown otherwise, that Watson would fall apart again if the pressure was turned up high enough.

Watson was asked who he thought was his biggest threat. Everyone expected him to say Nicklaus. "Myself," he said instead.

Sunday arrived, and Nicklaus did turn up the heat. He birdied the first hole, then birdied the second and sent a clear message to Watson and Crenshaw: he was lurking. Golfers talked about the feeling that emerged when Nicklaus's name started moving up the leaderboard. "People would always ask me, 'What's it like playing with Jack?'" Roger Maltbie recalled. "Well, you stand on the first tee. He knows he's better than you are. You know he's better than you are. He knows that you know he's better than you. And everyone watching knows he's better than you are. That's what it's like."

"You'd see Jack on the leaderboard," Johnny Miller said, "and you would think, 'Okay, you better make birdies.'"

Gary Player said, "He made you put more pressure on yourself. Everyone thought he put pressure on you, but no, you did that to yourself. Jack made you do that to yourself."

Nicklaus was aware of the effect. He often said that he did not try to intimidate other golfers, but that is semantics; he did intimidate other golfers, and he knew it. Miller got it exactly right: Nicklaus's imperviousness to pressure propelled golfers into going for birdies. And by going for birdies, they made mistakes.

Crenshaw broke first. He bogeyed the 2nd and 3rd holes, and it never really got better for him. "I can't explain it," he said of his crushing final day. "I'll learn to play someday."

Watson held up. One of the wonderful things about the Masters Tournament is that the layout turns the golf course into a giant soundstage. When someone makes a great shot, the cheers rattle through the pines and echo all over Augusta National. On a wild Sunday like this one, cheers and shrieks rose sporadically from different directions, like the sounds of neighborhood firecrackers on the Fourth of July. Nicklaus roars flared up at first, but they were soon matched by Watson cheers. Watson birdied four holes in a row and led Nicklaus by two shots going into the back nine.

His lead had disappeared by the 13th. He was standing in the fairway when he saw Nicklaus make a birdie putt to tie for the lead. It was here that something happened, something Watson would always be embarrassed to talk about. When Nicklaus made his putt, he celebrated. From where Watson was standing it looked like he was waving right at him. Taunting him.

Watson was outraged. From behind the ropes, Bruce Edwards (golfers had to use local Augusta National caddies then) saw his friend's face flush red with anger. Though Watson had trained himself not to show emotion, managing to hide just what all those close losses had taken out of him, he was still Ray Watson's son. That meant he knew when his manhood had been challenged.

"Yeah, I was mad," Watson said later. "And responding to a slight, well, that was just part of my makeup."

As it turned out, Nicklaus was not taunting Watson. He was acknowledging the fans. But Watson did not see it that way. He saw red. He blasted a 2-iron over the water and matched Nicklaus's birdie to take back the lead. He made another birdie at the 15th and went to the 16th tee tied with Nicklaus for the Masters lead.

And here Watson won the golf tournament. Forty years later, he would remember every emotion he felt then. He was panicked. He was acutely aware of gravity; his arms felt heavy, his legs felt heavy, his stomach pitched and turned. This was it. This was the moment he had been building toward since he was a child. "My . . . nerves were right here, just underneath the chin," he says, holding his hand at his neck. "I had a choice to either hit a hard six-iron or a three-quarter [effort] five-iron, and normally you want to hit the hard shot when you're under pressure. But I was swinging so well. I just said, 'I'm going to hit the five, and start it straight at the hole. Just go right at it.'"

In Watson's retelling of the shot, he closes his eyes and faces forward, as if watching an old movie in his mind. "I hit as perfect a shot as possible. Perfect. The ball when it came off the club face—I watched the ball in the air and I watched it come down, and literally, the pressure that was up to here just started to drain and drain. And I said, 'Man, if I can do this when the pressure is on, I've got it.'"

Watson had set up a short birdie putt, which he missed. But he felt different after that disappointment. The nervousness was gone. Doubt was gone. He felt what he called a "vacuum from pressure." All of the doubts he had about himself, all of the near misses that piled up, all of the pressure that comes with being tied with Nicklaus in the lead at the Masters, all of it drained away, like the opening of a clogged sink. At the 17th, he faced a downhill eighteen-foot putt that broke four inches left—a nasty putt. But Watson knew he was going to make it. And he did. He was swashbuckling Tom Watson again, the kid who knocked in putts from everywhere. And when he made that putt, the most surprising thing of all happened.

Nicklaus stood on the 18th fairway and carefully plotted a classic Nicklaus shot. The tournament was still tied, and he planned to hit a 6-iron twelve feet to the right of the flag. That would give him a good look at birdie, make his par assured, and force Watson to do what Nicklaus had made hundreds of golfers do: make no mistakes.

Then he heard the roar. He stopped for a moment and turned around. Watson had made birdie. Wait, Watson had made birdie? That meant he led the tournament now. That meant the par Nicklaus had planned might be good enough only for second place.

Roars like that had surrounded Nicklaus countless times before. But, he would say years later, he had never *heard* the roars the way he heard that one. "That's the only tournament in my life when I got flustered and couldn't regroup."

If Nicklaus had been clear-minded, as he usually was under pressure, he would have hit precisely the same shot he had intended. But instead he decided to aim for the flag and try to match Watson's birdie. It was exactly the sort of rash and cloudy thinking Nicklaus had inspired in everyone else. "I didn't need to do that. He still had to par the last hole."

Nicklaus hit the riskier shot fat, and the ball landed in the front bunker, the worst place he could have put it. He bogeyed the hole and fell behind two shots. When Watson made it to the fairway, he assumed Nicklaus was putting for par. He asked a gallery member, who said Nicklaus was putting for bogey. Watson didn't believe it and asked a tournament official closer to the green. When finally assured that he had a two-shot lead, he realized that he had done it. He had beaten Jack Nicklaus.

"There are a few shots that I really kick myself for, you know?" Nicklaus says. "That one is probably as big as any of them. . . . Iremember it like yesterday. I kicked myself all the way back to Palm Beach."

There were still a few details to hammer out after the tournament. Watson sought out Nicklaus to scold him for the taunt at the 13th hole. Nicklaus was shocked by the charge and immediately said, "Tom, I would never do that. I was just waving at the gallery." When he calmed down, Watson realized that this version of events made a lot more sense, and he sheepishly apologized to Nicklaus, who shrugged it off.

Nicklaus went into the interview room and was asked what he thought about Crenshaw's theory that while young golfers respected Nicklaus, they no longer feared him. He was about to answer when, from the back of the room, a voice spoke out. It was Watson.

"Let me answer that," Watson said. "I'm always afraid of this man."

"No, he's not," Nicklaus responded, a hint of a smile on his face. "He's not afraid of anyone. That's why he won."

SIMPLIFY

It boils down to one thought—a swing key, as Sam Snead would say. If you think about two things, that's too complicated.

TOM WATSON

I was a guy who could think about five or six things during the middle of a swing.

JACK NICKLAUS

Watson's friend, the Hall of Fame baseball player George Brett, would try an experiment with young hitters. He asked them to hold up anywhere from one to five fingers on one hand. At the same time, he told them to shout out a number between one and five. The complication: the two numbers had to be different. For instance, you could hold up two fingers and shout, "Five." Then you might hold up three fingers and say, "One." The challenge was to see how many times the hitter could hold up one number and shout out another.

Most people can't do it more than three or four times in a row unless they come up with a pattern. Brett's point: Think about one thing. Two is too many. He would say that, as a hitter, he had room for only one thought at a time. These changed over the years. One time the thought might be: Keep the hands back. Another, it might be: Don't lunge.

One thought worked. Two thoughts crippled him. Watson believes exactly the same thing, believes that singularity of thought is even more important in golf because golf is not a reaction game. The mind easily wanders. Is the takeaway too jerky? Is your head straight? Are you in balance? Is your right elbow tucked? Is your left arm straight? Are you shifting your weight? Are you swinging with your hands?

There is no limit to where a golfer's mind can drift. The writer John Garrity, who, like Watson, is from Kansas City, once went on a mission to improve his game by trying every available device and gimmick. He ended up destroying his game entirely because his mind was going in a thousand different directions. At the end of the experiment, Garrity found that he could barely even bring the club back. It took him years to repair the damage.

One thought. Watson suggests golfers start with something basic, like his father's advice: "Finish with your belly button facing the target." He says the thought forces you to turn your body toward the hole and naturally triggers numerous other positive movements.

Another possibility: "Accelerate through the ball." This came from Byron Nelson, who believed acceleration to be the most important part of any golf swing. Watson, even after he became a champion, would sometimes remind himself simply to accelerate through the ball, to hit the ball aggressively rather than swinging too carefully and cautiously.

"You think of one thing, and you get confirmation that the one thing works, and you stick with it," Watson says. "That's the plan. When that key stops working, you change that key and try to find something that does work."

Nicklaus agrees with Watson about keeping things simple, but he says that he had many thoughts when swinging the club:

"How many things I could think of, I don't know. But I would be thinking about my body relaxing, I might think about my head position to start with, how I take my hands away from the ball in the first twelve inches, where I want to set up at the top, how I want to change direction. . . . I could think of all those things as I was swinging."

When I tell this to Watson, he looks mildly surprised and then smiles. "But that's Jack Nicklaus."

HOLE NO. 9

Even in the Middle Ages, the linksland by the Firth of Clyde on Scotland's west coast looked like a golf course. The first time someone tried to turn the land into a golf course, the owner declined. That land was for hunting hares and rabbits. "With the sport of hare hunting so important," the owner wrote, "we must have land."

But the land that became Turnberry stubbornly evolved into a golf course anyway, a place for *gawf*, as the locals called it. The sheep chewed down the grass, the rabbits scratched at the earth, and sheep burrowed deeper to build beds; these became bunkers. The marram grass and fescue grew high, and these became rough. Even the earliest gawfers knew it was best to keep their balls out of the marram and fescue.

In Scotland golf was nature, nature was golf, and no place symbolized this symmetry better than the linksland that would become Turnberry. The local legend goes that Robert the Bruce, the warrior who led Scotland to independence, was born at Turnberry Castle in 1274. There are other claims to Robert's birthplace, but these are dismissed at Turnberry. There, cut into the rock that rises high above Turnberry, is what looks like the outline of a face, and no one doubts that it is the face of Robert the Bruce.

Turnberry was not officially turned into a golf course until the early part of the twentieth century, and by then Turnberry Castle was in ruins. A lighthouse built by the father and uncle of Robert Louis Stevenson had become Turnberry's most distinct man-made landmark. Off in the distance rose Ailsa Craig, a giant rock structure on which Catholics had hidden during the Reformation. On a clear day, Ailsa Craig looks close enough to touch, but there are few clear days at Turnberry. The local saying is "If you kin see the Ailsa Craig, it's gaun rain. If you kint see the Ailsa Craig, tis awready rainin.'"

The Royal and Ancient Golf Club of St. Andrews, the governing body that determines which courses get into the rotation to host the Open Championship, had concerns about giving Turnberry the 1977 Open. Turnberry's beauty was unquestioned, but the course was also remote. The R&A wondered if fans would be able to find the place.

Another thing: Turnberry had gone to war. During both World Wars, the course was used as training grounds for the Royal Flying Corps and Commonwealth Flying Units. This had only a limited effect during World War I; the planes were frail things, stitched together from wood and canvas, and did not require runways or landing strips. Planes landed directly on the fairways. Only weeks after the war ended, golfers played Turnberry again.

World War II proved a more daunting challenge. The planes were much bigger and heavier. Engineers built foot-thick concrete runways on top of fairways. Tanks rolled over Turnberry. That the golf course survived at all was due in large part to the stubbornness of the land. In places the course is so hilly that it simply defied being built over. Turnberry is also so infertile that it has almost no farming value. It is as if God had determined that Turnberry should be a golf course.

Still, after the war Turnberry was in such shambles and its grand hotel so dilapidated that most thought it would never reopen. The hero of Turnberry was a man with the perfect name: Frank Hole. He convinced the British government that it was in the nation's best interest to bring its golf courses back to life. A sixty-year-old golf course architect named Mackenzie Ross was hired to rebuild Turnberry, and he set about trying to return the land to its original beauty. His workers tore up the runways and covered the land with sand and topsoil. Then Ross waited for Turnberry to return to its natural state.

By 1977, when Watson and Nicklaus arrived for the Open Championship that would eventually be dubbed "the Duel in the Sun," the only remaining signs of war were a monument to the men who had died and a few slabs of runway where golf was not played.

This being Turnberry, everyone expected a wet and windy Open Championship. Instead the sun baked the greens brown, and the fescue and tall grasses were so thin and wispy that they barely troubled golf balls. Roger Maltbie had come to his first British Open fully prepared to be embarrassed by the bad bounces and fierce winds that mark links golf; instead he found a tame Turnberry that reminded him of golf courses back in America. "It was golf I was familiar with," he said. "And that was unexpected." Maltbie shot a 66 on the second day and led the Open going into the final two rounds. That too was unexpected.

What Maltbie remembered most clearly were the red bodies;

they were everywhere. The Scots were unprepared for the sunshine and warmth, and many took off their shirts. There were those who stripped down to their underwear. It was quite a sight, red-wine skin in every direction. "I've never seen people that sunburned in my life," he said.

Watson and Nicklaus shot matching 68s on the first day, 70s on the second, and were paired together for the Friday third round. They were a shot back, along with Hubert Green and Lee Trevino. It seemed as though every good golfer in the world was within a few shots of the lead. This, however, would not last. Soon it would be Watson and Nicklaus alone.

Nicklaus made his move right at the start of the third round. On the first hole, he hit an iron shot to three feet and made birdie. He birdied the 4th, the 6th, and the 7th to get to 6-under par. He was two shots clear and seemingly ready to pull away. There was a noticeable gasp around Turnberry as the name NICKLAUS moved to the top of leaderboards. Dust kicked up as spectators left whatever group they were following and ran toward Nicklaus so that they could glimpse the great man in full flight.

Watson too was playing well. He faltered at the 6th when his tee shot dropped in the sand. He hit an indifferent bunker shot and made bogey. But he made birdies at the 3rd, 4th, and 7th and felt he was within range of Nicklaus. Then lightning flashed across the sky. Watson and Nicklaus took cover in the rocks along the Firth of Clyde and waited for the weather to pass. Neither would remember saying a word.

"I sensed there was something special happening," Watson recalls. "It was certainly special for me. I was playing with the best golfer ever, and I was in contention at the British Open. Did I know what was coming? No. Of course not. I was just trying to win an Open Championship. But I knew it was special."

Nicklaus did not know yet. "I don't mean any disrespect to Tom, he knows that. But I didn't care what anybody else did. I felt like if I played my game, I'd have a good chance to win. I knew Tom was a good young player. There were a lot of good young players through the years."

If that sounds dismissive, well, Nicklaus was always respectful, always a gentleman, but he also could be dismissive. One of his favorite things to do during major championship weeks was open up the newspaper and see which of his competitors was complaining about the weather or the course conditions or anything else. He would then smile and mentally cross that player off the list of contenders. Those golfers who complained about stuff they couldn't control had already lost.

Watson saw a legend. Nicklaus saw another young gunslinger trying to take him out. When the sky brightened, Nicklaus birdied the 10th hole with a long putt. Watson did the same. At the 14th, Nicklaus hit a 7-iron too hard and watched the ball roll to the back of the green, forty feet from the hole. He missed a five-foot par putt, and his lead over Watson was just one shot.

On the 15th hole, Watson hit a beautiful 3-iron to the green and made a twenty-foot birdie putt. The two men were tied for the lead.

The biggest moment of that third day probably came at the par-5 17th hole. Nicklaus loved finishing rounds with a flourish. He took dead aim with the 2-iron and hit it so well that he listened expectantly for the sound of the crowd. The cheers hit him like confetti. The ball had rolled to within two feet of the cup. Nicklaus surely would make an eagle and take the lead of the Open Championship, perhaps by as many as two shots depending on what Watson did.

Here Nicklaus learned something about Tom Watson.

Nicklaus had thrown his dagger. It was the sort of shot that had broken golfers' wills for many years. But Watson pulled a 3-iron and hit a beautiful shot of his own to within fifteen feet of the hole. Nicklaus could not help but admire it.

They walked up to the green. Watson two-putted for birdie, and all that was left was the formality of Nicklaus making his eagle putt to take the lead. Instead he missed it. He hit the putt left and it rolled by. On the BBC broadcast Peter Alliss said, "Nicklaus looks almost embarrassed by that." Nicklaus quickly knocked in his birdie putt to tie Watson at 7-under par. That's how the third round would end. Watson and Nicklaus were three shots clear of the field.

"I was trying to make it a one-man tournament," Nicklaus would say with a touch of disappointment in his voice. Then he added, "So was Tom."

There are few things sportswriters like more than a rivalry. When reporters tried to coax Nicklaus into saying that a rivalry was budding with the young Tom Watson, Nicklaus quietly demurred. He was not yet willing to call Watson a rival. He said instead that it was "about the same as I've been facing for fifteen years against players like Trevino, Miller, Gary Player, Doug Sanders, Arnold Palmer and the rest down the line."

Watson, however, did not hide his enthusiasm for the fight. "I'll go against Jack tomorrow with respect, as I would with any other player," he told reporters. "I will be trying a little bit harder."

They were dressed as mentor and upstart. Nicklaus arrived at the 1st tee wearing navy blue slacks and a yellow sweater; he wore yellow on Sundays for a boy named Craig Smith, the son of Barbara's pastor, Bill. Craig had contracted bone cancer when he was eleven, and Jack had asked him his favorite shirt color. Craig said yellow, and Nicklaus wore yellow in the biggest moments, even after Craig died. That was six years before the Duel in the Sun.

Watson wore polyester double-knit pants with crisscrossing gold and green stripes, a wide white belt, and a lime green shirt. He would not remember consciously choosing that outfit for the day. He had a contract with Jantzen menswear, and he simply wore what they sent him.

"Jack was definitely more conservative than I was that day," Watson said.

"That was probably the last time I was more conservative than Tom," Jack replied.

In the movie *The Hustler*, Fast Eddie Felson, played by Paul Newman, is a small-town pool hustler with an unspoken ambition to become the best pool player in the world. To become the best, he needs to beat Minnesota Fats in a marathon round of straight pool. The first time they play, Felson overwhelms Fats with a barrage of trick shots and combinations. After a few hours, Felson has won so much money that Minnesota Fats considers giving up. Then he looks at Felson, sees that he is drunk and arrogant. Fats washes up, resets his mind, and wins back all of his money and then takes almost everything Felson has. The movie follows Fast Eddie's painful path to his rematch. At one point, he finds himself discussing the rematch with a gangster named Bert.

"How much do you think you'll need?" Bert asks him.

"A thousand," Eddie says.

"No," Bert barks, "three thousand at least."

Eddie looks at Bert with wide eyes.

"He'll start you off at five hundred a game, and he'll beat the pants off you," Bert says. "That's the way he plays when he comes against a man who knows the way the game is. He'll beat you flat four or five games, maybe more depending on how steady your nerves are. But he might, he just might, be a little scared of you. And that could change things."

Nicklaus began that final day at Turnberry determined to beat Watson flat and end all the drama. In golf, as in pool, that is how you play against a man who knows the way the game is. On the 2nd hole, Nicklaus hit his approach shot close and made birdie. Watson hit his approach shot off the green and made bogey. Just like that, Nicklaus led the Open Championship by two shots.

At the 4th, Nicklaus made a twenty-foot putt for birdie and Watson could not match it. Nicklaus was at minus-9, Watson at minus-6, and the rest of the golf world was far back in the rearview mirror. It seemed over.

And yet Watson again felt that strange calm he had felt the last two holes of the Masters. "Nobody wants to be down three to Jack Nicklaus," he said later. "But I honestly never had any doubt that I could catch him. My feeling there was like, 'Well done, Jack. Now it's my turn.'"

On the 5th hole, which the Scots call "Fin Me Oot," it was Watson's turn. He hit a wonderful approach shot and made a sixteen-foot putt for birdie. The lead was two. The crowd, so happy to be watching two men play golf this well, was huge and in motion. They were kicking up so much dust that Jack Boyd, a marshal that day and, later, the official historian of Turnberry, said that it looked like the golf course was on fire.

Watson and Fyles had very different ideas about a caddie's role in a golfer's life. Watson (and Nicklaus) saw a caddie's job this way: Show up on time, give accurate yardages to the hole, and offer moral support and the occasional advice on club selection. That's all. As Watson grew older and closer to Bruce Edwards, their bond did transcend the typical golfer-caddie relationship. Even with Edwards, though, Watson was clear: the golfer was in charge.

Fyles saw a caddie as more of a partner. He took personal pride in Watson's Open Championship in 1975. He believed he had played a vital role. The two never did come to an agreement on that, but they did come to an understanding: Watson handled the golfing, and Fyles handled the caddying. Something about their partnership brought out the best in each other.

On the 6th hole at Turnberry, Watson did something he had never done before and would never do again. He faced a tricky six-foot putt for par. He had to make it. He looked at the putt from about ten different angles, not typical for Watson, who usually played fast and loose. He just could not get a good read on how the ball would break. He turned to Fyles and asked, "What do you see?"

Fyles was stunned. Watson was one of the great putters in the world and, moreover, was fearless on greens. He never doubted himself. Until now. Fyles was shaking a little as he analyzed the putt. He then stammered, "Mister, it will move to the left just at the last."

Watson nodded. He stepped over the ball, waited over it a couple of beats longer than usual, and then knocked it in for par. He was still two shots back. As he walked by, he looked at Fyles for only a second and said simply, "Good line."

Watson hit his best shot of the week at the par-5 7th hole. He hit a driver from off the fairway, one of golf's most difficult and treacherous shots, a shot that can hook or slice a hundred yards off course, and he struck it just right. The ball rolled on the green. Nicklaus watched Watson's fantastic shot and then considered his own position. He was closer to the hole than Watson had been. He could have tried a similarly risky shot. But Nicklaus chose instead to hit a safe shot, the smart shot. Watson made birdie, Nicklaus par, and the lead was one.

On the next hole, Watson tied Nicklaus for the lead when he made a twenty-foot birdie putt that he had struck way too hard. If the ball had been even a touch off center, it would have rolled six or seven feet past the hole. This was the swashbuckling Watson, who putted boldly and utterly without fear. When the ball dropped in the hole, the sound of the gallery was like an explosion. But over the gallery Watson heard the voice of his father. Whenever young Tom had hit a shot that took a fortunate bounce, Ray would bark, "That was a lucky shot, not a good one." On the 8th hole at Turnberry, Tom could hear his father shout, "That was a lucky putt, not a good one."

Still, the match was all-square. The golf and the sunshine and tension, all of it was so wonderful that the elated Scottish fans became unhinged. People raced over the ropes that guard the course and began running on the fairway. Watson and Nicklaus were surrounded by the sunburned and lubricated masses. It was both fun and dangerous. Watson would remember feeling dazed, as if in a dream. The fans were all around him, shouting and patting him on the back, and he found himself using a few of the maneuvering skills that had marked him as a running quarterback in high school in Kansas City.

Nicklaus, as usual, kept his composure. And he put an end to the madness. He walked over to Watson and said, "We should stop until they get this under control." Watson agreed. Nicklaus then went over to some policemen and marshals and said, "This is getting out of control. We'll wait."

Nicklaus sat down on his golf bag. Watson walked over and

stood next to him. Together they watched people flutter about the golf course like young children playing their first soccer match. Off in the distance, Ailsa Craig reflected the sun. Nicklaus and Watson were leading the Open Championship, playing golf as well as it had ever been played, and they waited in silence on the 9th tee, by the sea.

THE TURN

Good caddies tell no tales, and Bruce Edwards was a good caddie. He caddied first for Watson when he was the best golfer in the world. Later he caddied for Greg Norman when he was, if not the best golfer, certainly the most interesting and gifted.

Norman, who grew up in Australia, played a brand of golf that boggled the mind. He could do everything. He drove the ball like Nicklaus, only straighter. He hit high iron shots like Johnny Miller. He had a magical short game like Watson. Norman had golden hair, an Australian accent, and a marvelous nickname: the Great White Shark. He won more money playing golf around the world than anyone ever had.

What Norman did not have, for some reason or other, was success in the major championships. In 1986 he led all four majors after three rounds; he won only one of them. The losses were spectacular and heartbreaking. At the Masters, Nicklaus himself came out of the past to beat Norman at age forty-six. At the PGA Championship, an unknown named Bob Tway holed out from the sand to beat him. And so on. This was Norman's lot in life; he lost major after major through bad luck, bad timing, or final-round collapses.

People would often ask Edwards to explain the difference be-tween Watson and Norman. Here were two talented men, two larger-than-life figures, and yet Watson won eight major cham-pionships while Norman won only two. Edwards mostly avoided the topic. Good caddies tell no tales. But one day, near the end of his life, Edwards spoke about the two men.

"I guess it comes down to this," he said. "When Greg hits a bad shot, he takes it very hard. He will say, 'Why didn't I get a kick left?' or 'Oh, that's the worst place I could have hit it,' or 'OK, there goes the tournament.' He's very hard on himself. And when Tom hits a bad shot, he will look at me, wink, and say: 'Just watch how I get out of this one.'"

TAKE YOUR LUMPS

Back when I started, I made an important rule for myself: Never follow a bad shot with another bad shot. Meaning if you had the option to play another risky shot after a bad shot, you better back off a little and take your lumps.

TOM WATSON

Most golfers want to fix their bad shots. That's the natural reaction. But, as Watson often says, the natural reaction is often the wrong reaction. Golf is an upside-down game. You hit down to make the ball go up. To score low is to place high. And sometimes hitting the ball right at the flag is about the worst thing you can do.

In golf, then, trying harder often leads to bad things. Watson believes the first and best way for an amateur golfer to lower his scores is to cut out the big numbers, to eliminate those triple bogeys, the snowmen, the round-wrecking double-digit scores. When he was a young player, he hit many wild shots, and he understood that such wildness would not allow him to last long on the PGA Tour. He simply had to reduce and then, as best he could, eliminate double bogeys.

He realized that the way to avoid double bogeys was to be sure he didn't hit two bad shots in a row. More to the point, he had to make sure not to hit two stupid shots in a row. Some nutritionists suggest that dieters give themselves one meal to splurge on anything they want: pasta, ice cream, chocolate, whatever. The key, they say, is that it must be one meal. There's only so much weight gain with one meal.

Watson applies this theory to golf. One bad shot can hurt you only so much if you surround it with smart ones. A bad drive can be salvaged with a sensible second shot. A shot into the woods can be countered with a solid recovery shot. A missed putt will cost you only one shot if you make the next one.

Watson's point is that scores are destroyed when golfers turn bad situations into worse ones. When I point out that it's more fun to try the risky shot than fix a mistake, he offers a sharp correction: "No. It's more fun to get a lower score."

HOLE NO. 10

When Nicklaus began playing professional golf, none of the top golfers knew the exact yardage of their upcoming shots. Such precision seems so elemental now, but for a hundred years or more caddies merely eyed the ball, eyed the flag, and offered a club that seemed best suited to cover the distance. Sam Snead, the man with perhaps the most beautiful swing in golf history, said he probably lost a half dozen tournaments because he used the wrong club at a critical moment.

In the late 1950s an amateur golfer with a mathematical mind named Gene Andrews came up with what in retrospect seems blindingly obvious: he calculated exact distances before he played his round. A better amateur golfer named Deane Beman (who would later become the commissioner of the PGA Tour) used this strategy to win two U.S. Amateur titles and six professional tournaments. In 1961 he was playing golf at Pebble Beach with a twenty-one-year-old Jack Nicklaus. "Why don't you try walking off the golf course?" Beman asked him. "Instead of guessing how far it is, why don't you just know exactly how far it is?"

"So I walk out," Nicklaus recalls more than a half century later, "and there's a pine tree on number one at Pebble Beach. I said, 'Okay,' and walked off one hundred thirty-eight yards to the front [of the green], one hundred sixty-one yards to the back. I put that on my scorecard."

He then measured the distance from a bunker on the right, the distance from a tree on the left, and so on. He went to every hole and meticulously stepped off the distances. He wrote them down on his scorecard. That week in the tournament he was under par in all twelve rounds he played.

Nicklaus had great natural talent for golf and undoubtedly would have been one of the best golfers even without Beman's small bit of advice. But getting exact yardages appealed to his meticulous mind. Soon after, he began to aim not for a nebulous "great round" but instead for a specific score, the score he believed would win the golf tournament.

"Jack would say, 'Okay, I need to go out there and shoot a sixty-eight today,'" Watson says. "And then he would go out and shoot a sixty-eight and win the tournament. I couldn't do that. I couldn't think of a number. But who really could? That's part of what made him Jack Nicklaus."

Here's a story about Nicklaus's mind at work: He once hired a caddie named Eric Veilleux, and in their first week together he reached his golf ball during a practice round and asked for a distance. Veilleux said, "It's about one hundred fifty-three." Nicklaus looked hard at him.

"Eric," he said, "we are not playing this game with 'abouts.' How far is it?'"

Veilleux gulped and said, "It's one hundred fifty-three."

Nicklaus nodded. "Okay. I don't want any 'abouts.' Because that is not what we are about."

Like Hogan and Bobby Jones before him, Nicklaus transformed golf from art to science.

The 9th hole at Turnberry is named "Bruce's Castle" because it is close to the ruins of the castle where Robert the Bruce may have been born. It is also in the shadow of the lighthouse built by Robert Louis Stephenson's father and uncle. When the fans finally calmed down and play resumed, Watson hit his poorest drive of the day and then, breaking his own rule of never following one bad shot with another, pulled his 1-iron shot into the left rough. He hit an indifferent chip shot and missed the par putt. It was, all in all, a dreadful hole, his worst in two days.

Nicklaus had his own problems on Bruce's Castle, and he faced a tricky twelve-foot putt to save his par. He stood over the ball, perfectly still, for a long time. Watson watched him closely. He and the other golfers knew that Nicklaus was not a particularly gifted putter, but he never seemed to miss an important putt. Something steadied him in the biggest moments. Nicklaus's caddy, Angelo Argea, once said that Nicklaus could enter worlds of focus that other golfers simply did not know existed.

Nicklaus made the putt. He remained 9-under par. Watson was 8-under. Nobody else in the field was under par at all.

Roger Maltbie, the California golfer who had led the Open Championship after two days, had fallen hopelessly behind, trailing Nicklaus by twenty strokes. Maltbie had no illusions about himself. He was a good golfer and had a good understanding of the game; later he would use that understanding to become a standout golf announcer. But he knew that he was no Nicklaus and no Watson. "You have to understand," he would say. "I was a mere mortal."

Maltbie is often asked about the Duel in the Sun because of

the minor role he played in it; he says that it came down to Nicklaus's science against Watson's art. Nicklaus's genius was his precision, his competence, his skill at choosing precisely the right shot for precisely that moment. He played exceedingly slowly, not because he moved slowly—even as a heavy young man he was a light-footed athlete who excelled at tennis—but because he took more time than anyone else to consider and align his shots. He never hit a shot before he was ready.

Watson, in contrast, was the turbulent artist. He was the fastest walker on tour; he almost ran to his ball. And when he got to the ball, he considered only a handful of variables and then hit. Fast and loose. He saw golf as a game in motion.

You could perhaps explain the difference between Nicklaus and Watson simply by describing their putting grips. Nicklaus held the putter with the lightest of pressure, the way a doctor might hold a scalpel. Watson held his putter so tightly that, at times, you could see the blood rush to his fingertips. Nicklaus tended to be conservative when he putted. Watson wanted to make all the long ones. "He would hole out from the most unforeseen places," Maltbie said. "In his heyday, there was nobody who hit putts the way he did. He ripped putts into the hole. Jack, in my view, just knew that he was inevitable. He would say, 'If I play the golf course, I'll probably get the lower score.' And he was right. Tom, I think, played more for the thrill of the moment. With Tom, anything could happen at any time."

The 9th hole nerves seemed to linger for Watson. On the 11th, a par-3, he dumped his tee shot into the sand and barely managed to save par. On the 12th hole, next to the monument dedicated to the airmen at Turnberry who died during the two World Wars, he again left his approach shot short of the green. He hit a nice putt from off the green to save par, but he knew pars would not be enough, not when Nicklaus was playing so well. Nicklaus had a twenty-two-foot putt for birdie and a two-shot lead.

Once more Watson watched in admiration as Nicklaus entered his own world. He bowed majestically, cocked his head slightly, and then stood motionless over the ball. If he made the putt—and the great lag putter was trying to make this putt—he might put Watson away once and for all. The stroke was perfect. The ball rolled toward the hole as if pulled by a magnet.

The television golf director Frank Chirkinian told his announcers before every big tournament, "The first person who says, 'The ball is in the hole,' will be fired. They can see the ball went in the hole." Yes, everyone could see the ball go into the hole. Nicklaus led by two. The Duel seemed over.

On the BBC broadcast Peter Alliss said, "One wonders who in the world can catch Jack Nicklaus two-up over six holes."

"How often," Herbert Warren Wind wrote, "does a golfer of Nicklaus' stature fail to hold on to a two-stroke lead as he drives down the stretch?"

"We have him," Nicklaus's caddie Angelo Argea would remember thinking.

Even thirty-five years later, Watson could not explain why he felt so calm. He could not explain why Nicklaus's sledgehammer putt did not discourage him. If it had been a year or two earlier, yes, no doubt, Nicklaus's sublime play might have broken his spirit. But something about the setting, the sun, the crowd, the rising dust made him feel immune to doubt. "I was just hitting the ball so well," he said. "It's hard to explain. Athletes talk about being in a zone. I would not call it a zone, but I just knew I was going to hit good shots. I was in control of my game."

That was it: he felt in control. Watson had never believed himself to be a choker, as the sportswriters described him. "I wasn't mentally tougher in 1977 than I had been in 1976 or 1975. Yes, I had more experience and had learned some things, but my competitive nature and my drive were no different. In 1977, though, I had a golf swing I could control."

The hole after Nicklaus seemed to end things was the 13th, called "Tickly Tap," meaning a tricky little putt. Watson made a delicate thirteen-foot putt to pull within one of Nicklaus. He almost tied on the 14th, just missing a six-foot birdie putt.

It was then that Watson had his moment. The 15th hole at Turnberry is a par-3 called "Ca-Canny," which means "Take care." Ca-Canny begins the golfers' return to the Turnberry Hotel. Watson did not take care on his tee shot. He hit the ball short and left. At first he thought he had hit into the bunker, a deadly place. Instead the ball was lying on the trampled-down marram grass, not much better than the bunker. Peter Alliss's tone became serious: "He'll do well to get down in two."

Nicklaus had his opening. He pulled his 4-iron and took dead aim. As soon as the ball was struck, he knew that he had done well. The ball landed on the front of the green and stopped twenty-two feet away from the hole. Watson would need all his skill just to make par. Nicklaus had a shot at making birdie. He recognized that this was where he would win the golf tournament.

When Watson reached his ball he realized that his best bet was to putt it, even though it was not on the green. He then looked at the line, and the scene felt familiar. The ball was in flattened grass, and there was some burned-out grass between him and the golf ball. Yes, this might have been an exotic scene—on the west coast of Scotland, near the ruins of Turnberry Castle, across the sea from Northern Ireland—but in the end this was just a long putt straight out of his childhood in Kansas City, Missouri. How many times had he hit a long, winding, hilly putt on green and brown grass? Nicklaus could do so many things better than Watson, better than anyone, but this kind of shot, well, now they were on Tom Watson's playground. He saw the line to the hole as clearly as if it had been marked with a yellow highlighter. All he had to do was hit the putt at the right speed.

But he didn't. He hit the putt way too hard. He knew that as soon as he hit it. If the ball missed the hole, he would face a treacherous eight- or ten-foot putt coming back. But the ball didn't miss the hole. It hit the flagstick squarely and disappeared.

Years later Alfie Fyles told Frank Deford that he looked at Nicklaus after that crazy putt dropped and saw Nicklaus rock back as if clocked with a punch. Nicklaus himself said this: "What do I remember about Turnberry? A lot has faded. I remember that putt at fifteen, of course. I won't forget that."

Up to that moment Nicklaus had expected to win. But when he left his own putt short, the match was tied. And Nicklaus found himself face-to-face with an uncomfortable possibility: maybe he wasn't going to be the hero this time.

As Nicklaus and Watson stood on the 16th tee, the fans were frenzied, the air felt electric, and from that high point they could see the Turnberry Hotel off in the distance and, along with it, almost every peak and valley in all of western Scotland.

"This is what it's all about, isn't it?" Watson said.

"You bet it is," Nicklaus replied.

On the 16th hole, both men left their birdie putts inches short, so they remained tied going into the final two holes. The 17th, a par-5 called "Lang Whang" (Long Whack), was a fairly easy birdie hole, and an eagle was very much a possibility. Nicklaus seemed to have had eagle assured the day before, but he missed a three-foot putt.

Watson hit a magnificent drive down the center of the fairway. Nicklaus hit his even better, and his ball rolled twenty yards past Watson's. "Massive drive," Alliss announced. They were both in an ideal position to set up eagle putts.

Watson hit first and hit well, leaving his ball about twelve feet from the hole. Now Nicklaus. His swing felt good, but for some reason—a reason he never did pinpoint—the contact was a little off and the ball coughed, wheezed, and dropped into the right rough. There were groans. The play from both players had been so close to perfect that this bit of humanity seemed out of place. Now it was Watson who underestimated his opponent. "I've put a nail in his coffin, haven't I, Alfie?" he asked his caddie.

Nicklaus studied his chip. For all his golfing genius, he was never viewed as a great chipper. But this time he displayed a marvelous touch, chipping the ball through the rough and rolling it to within four feet of the hole. In the din that ensued, Watson looked at his opponent with an expression that seemed to say, "Oh yeah, I forgot, you are Jack Nicklaus." Watson promptly ran his eagle putt a couple of inches past the hole, and all that seemed left was the formality of the two men making birdies and heading to the 18th still tied.

But four-foot putts are never formalities, not even for the best golfers. "What a horrid length," Alliss told his audience, and on television people saw Nicklaus do something he almost never did: second-guess himself. He had read the putt as straight in, no break either way, but something about the way Watson's putt had moved bothered him. Watson's putt had turned slightly, and this meant that his own putt might break a touch to the right. He looked at the line again; he could not see any break there. But Watson's putt had definitely moved.

In the end, he played his putt based on Watson's putt, aiming just left of the hole with the expectation that it would break right and drop in. He hit it just where he aimed. But the golf ball did not break right.

The sound from the crowd was a moan, some mixture of agony and disbelief. Nicklaus's miss was like being woken from a good dream. Watson tapped in his own birdie putt and found himself in a place he had not been the entire tournament. He was in the lead by himself, one clear of Nicklaus.

The 18th hole is a par-4 called "Ailsa Hame," which translates loosely as "the home hole" or simply "home." The green is in the shadow of the grand old hotel, making it one of the lovelier finishing holes in the world. Watson hit his 1-iron down the left-center of the fairway, putting the ball in ideal position. Nicklaus understood his task: he had to make birdie and hope that Watson did not.

Nicklaus reached for his driver. He had not used a driver on this hole all week, but these were desperate times. At the 1970 Open Championship, he had taken off his yellow sweater, pulled a driver, and ripped a mammoth drive that inspired the columnist Jerry Izenberg to later say, "Only gravity kept it on this earth." This time Nicklaus kept his sweater on, but the theme was the same. He unleashed the biggest swing he had. The instant after contact he knew that he had hit it poorly. The ball sliced way right into the area guarded by gorse bushes. Anticlimax drained the air at Turnberry. The Duel was over.

Watson walked over to Nicklaus's ball. It was resting two inches from the gorse—in other words, two inches from being unplayable or, as Scottish golfers say, "dead." Funny thing about those Scots: when they use the word *dead* in golf they can mean it in two diametrically opposite ways. A ball that is hit into so much trouble that there is no hope of making par is called dead. But a ball hit so close to the hole that a toddler could not miss putting it in is also called dead or, more colorfully, "stone dead."

Nicklaus's ball seemed to be the first kind of dead. It was so close to the gorse that Watson did not see much chance for Nicklaus to get the ball anywhere close to the green. But he would not underestimate Nicklaus again. He walked to his ball and faced a shot of about 180 yards. This would normally be a 5-iron shot for Watson, but Fyles handed him a 7-iron instead.

"What?" Watson asked in surprise. He looked toward the hole and recalculated the distance in his mind and then looked back at Fyles as if he were mad. Fyles nodded. He believed it was a caddie's job to see what the golfer could not see. "The way your adrenaline's pumpin', Mister . . . ," he replied, leaving the rest unsaid.

Watson nodded and took the 7-iron. He then hit the shot that would replay in his mind again and again, guiding him in good times, holding him steady in bad. His 7-iron soared onto the green. To Watson it looked like a piece of art against the sky. The ball hit softly and rolled to thirty inches from the cup.

Stone. Dead.

"Elementary, my dear Watson!" Peter Alliss pronounced it, and the exhausted crowd let out its loudest cheers of that incredible day. They would not stop cheering until Watson held up his hands. Then it was quiet for Nicklaus to play his shot.

Nicklaus selected a 7-iron and decided his only chance was to swing with all his might and, to use a Scottish word, *howk* the ball out. For 150 years, "tattie howkers" were young people hired to harvest potatoes in Scotland. There is no King's English equivalent. To howk potatoes means more than simply muscling or pulling them out of the ground; howking requires a summoning of strength and will that defies translation.

"Here comes the great man," Alliss announced, and Nicklaus pulled back his 7-iron and howked the ball out. The ball somehow rolled up on the green. It was impossible. Scottish fans raced to the hole in the ground that Nicklaus had gashed and dropped coins in as an offering to Turnberry and the golf gods in exchange for one more great Nicklaus putt.

Turnberry was chaos, fans rushing in from all sides to surround the green. Someone knocked over Fyles, and his wrist began swelling up before he and Watson reached the green. When they did get there, Watson saw his ball was even closer than he had expected. And Nicklaus's ball was thirty-two winding feet away.

"We've got him now, Mister," Fyles said.

Watson paused. Only a few moments earlier he had been certain that Nicklaus was done. Now he seemed to be thinking of something else.

"You know," Watson said suddenly, "I believe Jack is going to make this putt."

Fyles looked at his man.

"Yes," Watson said. "I expect him to make this."

"Fine, and so you make yours," Fyles ordered.

But Watson was barely listening. He was in the moment, and the moment felt like a movie, a perfect movie, the blue skies and the fading sun, the sunburned people all around, the beautiful hotel. Yes, he knew, really knew, that the greatest golfer who ever lived was about to make an impossible putt after an impossible shot. Then Watson would have to make his little putt to win the Open Championship. Yes, this was a movie, and the only question was which one of them would get the girl at the end.

Nicklaus did make his birdie putt. Of course he did; on this day it could not have ended any other way. He cracked his putt hard, and it broke right to left and dropped smoothly in the hole. All day the Scottish fans had been on the brink of hysteria, and this absurd and wonderful putt sent them over the edge. They whooped and leaped and hugged and cried as if it were Scottish Independence Day. Only when Nicklaus raised his arms did they become silent.

Watson had a two-and-a-half-foot putt for the Open Championship. It is tempting, for dramatic purposes, to say that his short putt looked impossibly long after Nicklaus made his magical putt. But both men knew he would make it. He stood over the ball for only a couple of seconds and then knocked it in to win the Duel in the Sun.

"My putt didn't really make that much of a difference because he wasn't going to miss that putt either way," Nicklaus said. "I mean, don't get me wrong: that was a neat putt to make. I think a lot of people enjoyed it, including me. . . . But whether I make it or not, it doesn't matter. When Tom hit that great shot into the eighteenth, he won the golf tournament."

Nicklaus walked over and put his arm around Watson. If Watson had spoken his heart at the 16th tee, Nicklaus spoke his heart now: "I'm tired of giving it my best shot and not having it be good enough."

Watson could think of nothing to say. Nicklaus had beaten the Open scoring record by seven shots. Watson had beaten it by eight. Nicklaus had beaten third-place Hubert Green by a full ten shots. Watson had beaten Green by eleven.

"I won the golf tournament," Green would tell reporters. "I don't know what course Tom and Jack were playing."

Nicklaus felt the sting of losing the Duel in the Sun, of course, but there were no regrets like there had been at Augusta earlier in the year. He felt he gave away the Masters. At Turnberry, Watson beat him. "I never minded that," Nicklaus said. "If you prepare properly, you've not done something stupid, you play well, and you get beat, then the guy just played better than you."

Years later Barbara Nicklaus was looking for a name for a cookbook they were writing together. "What was that you said to Tom after he beat you at Turnberry?" she asked.

"Well done," he said.

"Right," Barbara said, and that's what they called the cookbook.

That night, when Jack and Barbara Nicklaus walked into the Turnberry Hotel dining room, everyone stood and applauded so long that Nicklaus felt tears in his eyes.

At the same time, Dan Jenkins, *Sports Illustrated*'s golf writer, was working on his story. The last three paragraphs went like so:

> He could only watch as Watson tapped in from two feet.
>
> "I just couldn't shake him," Nicklaus said later to a group of friends.
>
> With that, he looked off in thought with something of the expression of an aging gunfighter. He did not say he had been expecting someone to come along one of these years. But the look seemed to indicate he had finally met him.

A little later, Tom and Linda Watson walked into the dining room, and everyone again stood and cheered. In the afterglow

Watson felt as if in a wonderful fog. They ate their dinner and then went into the ballroom and danced to "Blue Skies," Ray Watson's favorite song. When they returned to their room, there was champagne waiting, and they looked out the window as the light faded. The sound of a solitary bagpipe filled the evening. Watson cried as the sun set over the Firth of Clyde.

BE LUCKY

If you think yourself unlucky, you'll have bad luck. There's no scientific explanation for it, but it's a cold, hard truth in golf. That's one reason why bad bounces never bothered me as much as they did some people. The second you start thinking of yourself as a victim, you've had it.

TOM WATSON

You've heard this joke before: A golfer is playing the 18th hole in a big match, and he slices his tee shot way to the right. It rolls toward a creek. But before the ball can get to the water, it hits a tree and takes a wicked bounce left, where it settles into the middle of the fairway.

The golfer walks to the ball and tries to hit a high 7-iron that will land softly on the green; instead he tops the ball and it somehow rolls down the hill, snakes between two bunkers, and rolls on the green to about six feet from the cup.

The golfer goes on the green, studies his putt, then hits it too hard and too much to the left. The ball hits the left part of the hole and spins all the way around the cup before popping out about two inches from the cup.

"Come on!" the golfer shouts. "Can't I get a break here?"

The saying goes that you make your own luck, but Watson

thinks the concept is even more streamlined. He believes that the best golfers *feel* lucky. They feel something good will happen when they swing the golf club. They feel that one bad bounce—and there will always be bad bounces—will be outnumbered by two good ones.

This isn't some kind of "May the Force be with you" Yoda thing he's talking about. Watson is certainly not one to go on about Zen and the Art of Golf. He just believes that unlucky golfers, those who see themselves that way, are inevitably poor golfers. They rage at the bad breaks. They lose focus when things go wrong. They feel sorry for themselves when a well-struck shot does not yield the right result. They play negatively.

And the opposite must be true too. Watson does not know if the bad bounces and good bounces have evened out for him over the years. He doesn't see it quite that way. The game is not one of good and bad bounces. That's why the joke resonates. Let's say you hit two shots exactly the same. One hits the first cut of rough and takes a hard kick into a ditch and is blocked by a tree. The other kicks hard left and ends up in the fairway. Which is the lucky shot? The second one, right? Well, not necessarily. You could walk up to your ball in the fairway and dump the next shot in a pond in front of the green. If your ball is blocked by a tree, you might play a smart shot back into the fairway, hit a magnificent third shot, and make a par-save that sparks the best round of your life. Luck, in golf and in life, is not always obvious. Sometimes luck depends on how much you believe.

HOLE NO. 11

There was no riding off into the sunset for Watson and no glorious final scene for Nicklaus after the Duel in the Sun. The next day they flew to Boston, where they played in a tournament called the Pleasant Valley Classic. Watson played uninspired golf, Nicklaus played better, and Raymond Floyd won. Golf and life went on.

Writers began to write subtle obituaries for Nicklaus's career. He was thirty-seven and had now lost twice to Watson, who was ten years younger and ascending. Nicklaus found these eulogies premature and silly, but he did not talk about them much. There was nothing to say. He knew the talk would end only when he won his next major.

As for Watson, he was in demand. Writers from all over the world, swept away by his audacious play, rushed to Kansas City to find out about this new Nicklaus. "What makes Tom Watson tick?" they asked, a question the Stanford psychology major found tedious. He politely answered some questions and politely declined to answer others. He did not like it when reporters presumed to know him. One asked a softball question: Would you rather win the U.S. Open or a million dollars? Everyone who knew Watson knew how much he wanted to win the U.S. Open, so the answer seemed obvious. Instead Watson said, "Well, that's a loaded question. You want me to say the U.S. Open. If I was having trouble making ends meet, I might take the money and run."

The writers found contradictions. They had long described Watson as a grown-up Huckleberry Finn or Tom Sawyer, but the more they talked to him, the less that narrative fit. Watson's personality lacked Twain's mischievousness. He was serious and driven. Back when he was a running quarterback in high school, teammates had called him "Huckleberry Dillinger."

He was, at heart, Ray Watson's son. The younger version of Tom Watson rebelled against his father's Kansas City conservatism. Once, when Tom was nineteen, he was playing in the Western Amateur in Rockford, Illinois. He made a joke about Rockford not having much nightlife. He thought of it as a harmless joke, but as soon as his quote appeared in the newspaper, his hotel phone rang. The instant he picked up he heard an outraged Ray growl, "What's this about nightlife?"

By the time Watson beat Nicklaus in the Duel, though, he was a lot like his father. He had settled in Kansas City rather than move to a state with better weather, like Florida or California. And he did not just live in Kansas City; he saw himself as a son of Kansas City. He followed Kansas City's sports teams. He passionately argued about Kansas City politics. He ate often at Kansas City's famous barbecue restaurant, Arthur Bryant's. He was in many ways the cliché of a midwesterner: friendly but private, accommodating but distant, Republican but with many Democratic friends, principled but opinionated. He was as likely as anybody to say, "Hot enough for you?" when the Kansas City sun beat down. Reporters found that Watson would answer questions bluntly and honestly, but he would not tread beyond the walls of the question. He stopped as soon as the question was answered, like a driver slamming on the brakes. He preferred silence to small talk.

The Watson smiles told a story. There were two smiles, the first a broad and genuine expression of joy. That smile was for close friends and family. It was the smile he had when singing nursery rhymes to his daughter Meg as he rocked her to sleep. In public, he wore a harder smile. This was the smile that photographers captured through the years. It was tight-lipped and secretive. When he missed a putt, he would smile. When he hit a bad shot, he would smile. When he came upon a group of reporters after a bad round, he would smile. Edwards thought that smile was Watson's defense mechanism, a shield. Of course he never said that to Watson. Few things irritated Watson more than being psychoanalyzed.

In the end, the writers decided almost unanimously that Watson was just boring. The details they uncovered about him—that he kept up with current events, smoked cigarettes, was a family man, practiced a lot—fell flat on the page. Will Grimsley, the Associated Press columnist, once referred to the new generation of golfers as "Lanny Watson and Tom Wadkins," purposely conflating Watson with fellow pro Lanny Wadkins to reflect how little Watson stood out from the crowd. Others wrote more directly about how colorless he was. Professional golf, perhaps more than any other spectator sport, is propelled by the charisma of its best players. The dashing presence of Arnold Palmer had taken golf out of the country clubs and into the mainstream. The presidential demeanor of Jack Nicklaus sold suits to businessmen of America. What did Tom Watson bring?

He had principles. He had turned down numerous endorsement deals because he didn't believe in the products. He was such a stickler for golf's rules that he would write a book explaining them. When they were speaking on the record, his fellow golfers spoke blandly about his work ethic and skill around the greens; on background, they might mention that he was a bit of a scold and know-it-all. His wife, Linda, sometimes revealed a few small personal details, such as how hard he took losing and how sentimental he could be when the cameras were not around. The stories about Watson read very much alike.

"How does one get to be a colorful man?" he asked John Underwood for a *Sports Illustrated* story on his blandness. And then, sounding very much like his father, he asked, "Is it colorful to throw your clubs and curse little kids?"

Watson's glory years, when he was the best golfer in the world, were a montage of long putts holed, iron shots bobbing around flagsticks, long drives sailing into blue skies, cash registers ringing. Golfers need flaws in their games to give them humanity. Hogan missed a lot of putts and so did Snead. Palmer and, later, Phil Mickelson were often wild and needed miraculous shots to save themselves. Even Nicklaus had trouble chipping.

At his peak Watson did everything brilliantly. He had an exhaustive variety of shots; all those hours on the practice range had trained him to move the ball right to left or left to right with equal precision. He could punch it low, soar it high, power it out of the rough, pick it clean. His short game was unparalleled, his putting uncanny. "Every time I played with him," Gary Koch said, "he would make three or four putts of twenty feet or longer. He just expected that. He had so much positive energy in his putting. You hear about golfers willing the ball into the hole. Tom willed the ball in the hole again and again. I never saw him tentative around the green. Never."

The only thing that bogged down Watson in those days, Nicklaus said, was his perfectionism. He could not stop tinkering, could not stop adjusting. Watson did not try to hit a good shot; he wanted the perfect shot. "Tom loved trying to fashion a shot that was just right for the moment," Roger Maltbie said. "Sometimes he didn't pull it off, but he never stopped trying."

In 1979, for instance, Watson completely refashioned his swing in preparation for the U.S. Open at Inverness in Ohio. He was by far the best golfer in the world that year. His swing, in the words of Herbert Warren Wind, was "so geometrically correct that he could not fail to split the fairways off the tee and cover the flagsticks with his irons." Even so, he had yet to win the U.S. Open. He changed his swing to deal with Inverness's tight fairways. But the strategy backfired; he missed the cut.

"I do tend to think too much," Watson admits. "The funny thing is that when I'm playing well, I would say I play ninety percent by feel. You have to feel the shot. When I'm not playing well, it's usually because I'm not playing by feel."

Or, as the writer Dan Jenkins puts it, "Tom and Jack's games were so different. Jack was so calculating. Tom was, 'Hit it quick before your mind messes you up.'"

When Watson's mind did not mess him up, he was a marvel. "He makes golf, the exacting art of hitting a stationary ball from a stationary stance, seem as simple as stirring coffee," Wind wrote in *The New Yorker*. Watson put a static game in motion. He would hit his drive, look up to be sure his ball was on the right trajectory, and then stride down the fairway as if being pushed by the wind. His caddie Bruce Edwards was a fast walker (it was one of the reasons they got along so well), but even he sometimes had to break into a jog to keep up. When Watson reached the ball, he took almost no time at all. One practice swing. Two waggles.

Then hit. And with the ball in the air, he broke into that fast walk, that mysterious smile on his face, like a child racing off to search for Easter eggs.

In the years after the Duel, Watson won the PGA Tour's Player of the Year award four times in a row, something even Nicklaus never did. In 1980 he became the first golfer to win a half-million dollars in a single year. Nicklaus told reporters, "He thinks as well as anyone. . . . When you face Tom Watson you know he's not going to give it away." Nicklaus was saying of Watson what golfers had once said of Nicklaus.

And Watson had begun to display something about his character: he was at his best when conditions were at their worst. In 1979, at Nicklaus's Memorial Tournament, a bizarre spring storm roared through Columbus. Winds blew up to thirty miles per hour, icy rain fell, and the windchill dropped into the teens. On the second day of the tournament, almost half of the field failed to break 80. Even Nicklaus, who never liked talking about the weather, commented that by the time he reached the 18th hole he could no longer feel his hands. Only one golfer in the field broke 70.

"It wasn't all that bad out there," Watson told the press after he shot his 69. He smiled that Watson smile. He won the tournament.

"Tom understood—and I think I understood this too—that the worse the conditions, the more golfers you could cross off the list as contenders," Nicklaus said. "I think Tom loved playing in the rain and wind because he knew he would handle it better than anyone."

Watson confirmed this. "I don't like playing golf on sunny days."

• • •

Watson did not fall in love with links golf, really fall in love with it, until after he had won three Open Championships. In 1981 he went on a trip to Great Britain with his friend and the former president of the USGA Sandy Tatum. They had both attended Stanford, though some thirty years apart. Tatum, unlike Watson, had won an NCAA title.

Tatum was as responsible as anyone for the fierce conditions at the 1974 U.S. Open, the one that became known as the "Massacre at Winged Foot." That was where Watson first gained national notice, and also where he first built a reputation as a choker. Tatum famously said that those conditions were not meant to embarrass the best golfers but to identify them. Watson told Tatum he admired the poetry of the words. He didn't agree with them, not when it came to Winged Foot, but he admired them.

Before the 1981 Open Championship they went to Prestwick Golf Club, which had played host to the first eleven Open Championships, beginning in 1860. They went to Royal Troon, where Watson would win the fourth of his Open Championships, and they went to Ireland's Ballybunion, a course Watson would call one of his favorites in the world. Finally they went to Royal Dornoch in eastern Scotland, a club along the Dornoch Firth. Locals claimed that people had played golf at Dornoch as far back as the 1600s, and records show that even then people complained that young men in Dornoch should be spending more time working on their marksmanship and less time on frivolous gawf.

The sun was shining brightly as Watson and Tatum played their round on Dornoch's old links course, designed by golf's first legend, Old Tom Morris. When they finished, they went inside and drank some bitters. A small ceremony was held, and

Watson was named an honorary member. It was all very quaint and touching.

Then Watson heard rain splashing against the window. He looked outside and saw nothing but gray clouds and the blurry lines of hard rain. The wind was gusting. He smiled, the real smile, and caught Tatum's eye. "You want to play?" he asked.

"I'll organize the caddies," Tatum replied.

They put on their rain suits, and by the time they reached the 1st tee the wind was howling at thirty or forty miles an hour, blowing the rain sideways. They played eighteen holes and Watson played terribly. He remembered that as the only time that Tatum ever beat him in a match. But there was something magical about it.

When they got to the 16th hole, Watson turned to Tatum and said, "You know what, Sandy? This is the most fun I've ever had playing golf."

LEARN HOW TO LOSE

You don't put yourself in a position to lose. If you do that, you have a good shot of winning. That has been my philosophy through the years.

JACK NICKLAUS

Nicklaus says he learned his most important golf lesson when he lost the U.S. Open at Cherry Hills in Colorado. He was twenty years old, and he went into the final round three shots off the lead and five shots ahead of the world's best golfer, Arnold Palmer. He was paired with Ben Hogan; that was the day that Hogan said he had played with a boy who would have won by ten shots if he had any idea what he was doing.

Nicklaus agrees: "If I had known how to win, I would have won. But you don't know how to win when you start. You have to learn how to lose before you learn how to win."

He explains: There are intense emotions that people go through when they are under pressure. There is nervousness. There is fear. There is something like giddiness. There is also adrenaline. The mind races and jumps to memories and images that may or, more likely, may not be helpful. Making sense of these emotions takes experience.

But the biggest lesson Nicklaus picked up from Cherry Hills was not how to control his own emotions but instead to remember that everyone else was feeling the same pressure: "You learn that coming down the stretch, everybody is having the same problems you are. They're going to make mistakes. Sometimes a golfer like Tom or Lee Trevino just beat me. I played my best and they won. That never bothered me because I knew, most of the time, if I didn't beat myself, nobody would beat me."

This is what he means by "learn how to lose before you learn how to win." At Cherry Hills he learned how to lose; that is, he learned what his instincts were when under pressure. He played too aggressively; he worried too much about what Palmer was doing; he overestimated his competitors' nerve. He sees this sort of panic in weekend golfers. We hit silly shots because we are convinced our competitors will make birdies or pars. We go for broke when a conservative shot would give us a much better chance to win.

Nicklaus brings up the 1993 Masters. That year a good but not great golfer with a great golfing name, Chip Beck, trailed Bernhard Langer by three shots going into the par-5 15th hole. Beck was not a long hitter, and on his second shot he faced a 236-yard shot over water and into a breeze. To most of the people watching, he had no choice but to go for the green and give himself an eagle shot. Instead he decided to lay up.

There was an immediate backlash. Ken Venturi, announcing the Masters for CBS, said that Beck was "protecting second place," another way of saying he was not trying to win. Many sportswriters offered the same criticism. Beck ended up second, four shots behind Langer, and he was puzzled and stung by the reaction. "I know my game," he said. "It was 236 to the front, I was into the wind, and I had a downhill lie. I just don't have that shot."

Nicklaus said he never spoke with Beck about it, but he agreed with him: "He did absolutely the right thing." Beck hit the shot that would not lose him the golf tournament. He had no idea what Langer would do over the final four holes. "You don't win golf tournaments by hitting miraculous shots that you are not capable of hitting," Nicklaus says. "You lose golf tournaments that way."

"Remember," he adds, "most golfers self-destruct."

HOLE NO. 12

Age plays tricks on the golfer's mind. In other sports, baseball, for instance, players can fool themselves for only so long. The greatest baseball hitters find that one day they can no longer catch up to the fastball. You cannot kid yourself when you swing and miss pitches that you once hit on a line.

In golf, though, there are no fastballs to alert the players that their time has run out. Hogan played his best golf after he turned forty. Snead still hit beautiful golf shots well into his fifties. And at thirty-eight Nicklaus played magnificently at the Open Championship in 1978. That was at St. Andrews, home of the Royal and Ancient Golf Club.

Watson led that Open Championship going into the final round, one shot ahead of Nicklaus. Then, literally and figuratively, the wind shifted. When Nicklaus woke up on Saturday morning, he saw that the wind had turned; it would now blow into the golfers' faces as they began the round. Nicklaus was elated. This had been the wind direction when he won the Open Championship in 1970 at St. Andrews, the year he took off his yellow sweater at the 18th hole. He knew exactly what to do because he had done it before.

Watson did not cope well with the new wind; he made four straight bogeys on the front nine. The other contenders, including Ben Crenshaw, Tom Weiskopf, and a talented young Englishman named Nick Faldo, also faded away.

In the end, Nicklaus found himself contending with a relative unknown from New Zealand named Simon Owen, who had never before made the cut at an Open or any other major championship. That day, though, Owen played inspired golf. He chipped in from twenty-five yards away on the 15th hole to take the lead by a shot. Nicklaus later admitted that for a moment he flashed back to Turnberry, to the Duel in the Sun, and wondered if some young golfer was going to take another Open Championship away from him. Then he reminded himself: Simon Owen was not Tom Watson. On the 16th, Owen hit the ball over the green, and Nicklaus hit his shot to within six feet of the flag. On the 17th, St. Andrews's famous Road Hole, Owen hit his ball onto the road behind the green. Nicklaus won by two shots.

"I feel super. . . . Just give me a moment to calm down," Nicklaus said to reporters after it ended. They were surprised to find his voice choking with emotion. This was his first major championship in almost three years. *Sports Illustrated* named him Sportsman of the Year. Nicklaus proclaimed that he was now playing the best golf of his life.

And right after leaving St. Andrews, his game fell apart and he gave serious thought to giving it up. Age does play tricks on a golfer's mind.

Watson and Nicklaus were friendly in these days, but they were not friends. They could not be friends, not yet, not when they both still wanted to be the world's best golfer. They played brilliantly together in team golf events, never losing a match in the Ryder Cup, and they often played practice rounds together before tournaments began.

"I was still studying Jack and how he played golf courses," Watson says. "I wanted to see how he negotiated a course. And he was free with his information. I mean, I would ask him, 'What club did you hit there and why did you hit it there?' We would discuss strategy. He wasn't secretive."

Nicklaus fed off Watson's boundless energy: "In Tom, I saw someone who was focused entirely on winning. He was a lot like I was when I was younger. He reminded me a lot of myself in those early years. I was not the kind of person who worried about anyone else on the golf course. But I think it was good for me to be around Tom, to be around someone who cared that much."

They clearly were going in different directions. Watson won five times in 1978, five more in 1979, seven times in 1980. He contended at almost every major. Nicklaus spent less and less time on his game. He had a growing family. He had business interests all over the world. He had already won so much. His victory at the 1978 Open was his fifteenth professional major championship. How many more did he really need to win? What was left to prove?

Johnny Miller is convinced that Nicklaus had passed his prime before Watson began winning. He believes that by the late 1970s Nicklaus was winning more on guile and durability under pressure than on golfing brilliance. "Don't get me wrong, he still had a lot of game when he went up against Tom. Jack had a longer prime than any golfer who ever lived. But I would say the heart of his prime was [the] first part of the 1970s, when he could do just about anything on the golf course."

Nicklaus disagrees. "I don't think about it like that. My goal was to keep getting better. But I would say that I thought much better in my late thirties. I understood my game better. I knew what it took to win. I probably wasn't hitting it as far, but I would say that at St. Andrews in 1978, I played the finest tee-to-green golf I ever played at a major championship."

There is a technical reason that explains why Nicklaus's golf game disintegrated after St. Andrews. And it did disintegrate. He did not win a tournament in 1979, the first time in his professional career that he went a year without winning. Reporters theorized that he wasn't playing enough or had become fat and happy. But Nicklaus knew the real reason: his swing had lost its depth.

Nicklaus was a pioneer in what teachers call the upright swing. Hogan had a flat swing: he would bring the club back on a very low trajectory, so his hands on the backswing never rose above his right shoulder; he then swung on a shallow plane, almost like a baseball swing. Snead had what many still believe to be the most beautiful golf swing, and he too had a flat swing. Palmer had a flat swing.

Nicklaus, though, had been taught to swing upright; his hands went high above his right shoulder on the backswing. He and his teacher Jack Grout believed that an upright swing held the key to power because it allowed him to better use the strength in his arms and legs. The young Nicklaus hit golf balls farther than any great golfer had; the upright swing seemed the reason.

But as golfers age, something happens to their upright swing: it starts to get too vertical. This is the depth Nicklaus often talked about. As weekend golfers all over the world have found, if you are too steep on your golf swing—that is, if you swing the club up and then down without any horizontal depth—bad things happen. It is hard to hit the ball squarely. All power disappears. The ball begins slicing and hooking off course. This, in a general way, was what happened to Nicklaus. His swing began to lose depth. And he stopped winning.

That's when he thought about quitting. He was turning forty, ten years older than Watson and ten years younger than Palmer. He was at Robert Frost's two roads diverging in the yellow wood. Watson was at the height of his powers. Palmer was playing ceremonial golf because he could no longer compete. Nicklaus, in the middle, knew which road he would not take. "I don't want to play ceremonial golf," he told friends. "I don't want to shoot eighty and wave to the crowd."

So he decided that unless he could completely revamp and restore his swing and make himself a contender again, he would give up the game. He could imagine his life without golf. He had money; he had fame. He liked the business of designing golf courses. He liked being home and watching his sons play sports. And he wasn't sure he had enough energy and enthusiasm to radically change his golf swing. "I really did think about giving it up."

Watson never believed that for a second. "Do I think Jack really came close to giving up the game? Hell no. I guess he talked about it with Barbara and others. But he's too much of a competitor. There was never a doubt in my mind that Jack would come back stronger than ever."

Nicklaus asked his old teacher Jack Grout to come live near him, and together they worked seven days a week on adding depth to Nicklaus's swing. This required seemingly minor changes in his setup and backswing, but golfers know that there are no minor changes when it comes to a golfer's swing. Changing a golf swing even slightly is as uncomfortable as changing accents. "If you've ever had a long-ingrained golf fault, then made a mental commit-ment to fix it," Nicklaus would write in his autobiography, "I don't have to spell out how difficult doing so can be."

Nicklaus entered the 1980 golf season with his new swing. He finished second at the Doral-Eastern Open in Florida but fol-lowed that with his worst Masters performance in almost a quar-ter century. Again thoughts about retiring lingered. "Quit if you want to," his wife told him. "I don't mind. You have so many other things to do. But golf is such a big part of your life, I don't think you can be happy without it." A week before the 1980 U.S. Open, Nicklaus missed the cut in Atlanta.

Watson meanwhile was having a fantastic year, perhaps the best of his career. He won the first tournament he entered in San Diego and then won at Los Angeles. In April and early May he won three consecutive tournaments, the third of those being Nelson's tournament in Texas. It was the fourth time Watson had won the Byron Nelson Classic. Nicklaus finished forty-fourth.

Watson still had not won the U.S. Open, though. This seemed to be the year to break the spell. It was at Baltusrol in New Jersey, and Watson had honed his game to near perfection. He did not want to make the mistake he'd made the year before at Inverness, when he had put too much pressure on himself. Still, he could not pretend that the U.S. Open didn't matter.

"I put a lot of pressure on myself," he told reporters after he arrived in New Jersey. "I can't treat the Open as just another golf tournament because I don't see it that way. It's the Super Bowl, the NBA Championship and the Rose Bowl. It's impossible to say, 'It's just another tournament,' because it isn't."

On the first day he made a hole-in-one on Baltusrol's 4th hole. That seemed a good sign. He shot 1-over par, which in a typical

U.S. Open year would have put him right in contention. But this was no normal year.

Nicklaus shot a 63. "That was the best round I've shot in a long time," he told reporters, a typical Nicklaus understatement. There was something he did not say: his swing was back. All the hard work he had put in with Grout had crystallized. He was swinging the club like he had as a young man.

On the second day, Watson played more aggressively and finished with a birdie and eagle to get himself to 1-under par. Nicklaus played a solid but unspectacular round, and Watson trailed by only five shots. "I shot myself right back into the tournament," he insisted, and on Saturday he backed up his words by shooting a blistering 3-under par to pull within two shots of Nicklaus. Another duel seemed in the making.

Only this time there would be no duel. Nicklaus woke up Sunday morning and watched *Tom and Jerry* cartoons with his children. It was Father's Day, and even thirty-five years later he would remember how calm he felt. The Baltusrol crowds had been behind him like no crowds he could remember. The swing changes felt natural. The ball was going where he aimed.

Nicklaus took a two-shot lead into the back nine and then, like the younger version of himself, grabbed hold of the tournament. On every hole, he listened as the fans chanted, "Jack! Jack! Jack!" On the 17th hole, he stood over a twenty-two-foot birdie putt that he sensed would put the tournament away. He studied the putt for a long time, a Nicklaus amount of time, and he had this strangely self-aware thought: "This is exactly the kind of putt I make in moments like these." He knocked it in.

When he reached the 18th green, the crowd was frantic with joy. Again they chanted his name. On the manual scoreboard someone had written, "JACK IS BACK."

"I want to stop the retirement talk right now," Nicklaus said happily after he won. "I'm not going to retire. Perhaps I should. Perhaps I don't have any sense. If I wanted to go out with all the dramatics I would say goodbye. But I kind of like this crazy game."

Watson could not keep pace. He played well; his 4-under total would have won the U.S. Open the year before, and the year before that, and every year before that going back to Johnny Miller's virtuoso performance at Oakmont. In 1980, though, Jack was back. "I just shot 276, the fourth lowest score in the history of the U.S. Open," Watson said. "And I lost by four shots."

Years later Watson said that in his entire life there were five times he believed he would win a golf tournament before it began. He won four of them. When asked about the fifth, he shook his head. "I'm not saying what it was. But you can probably guess."

It was Baltusrol in 1980. He took several tournaments from Nicklaus. That was the one that Nicklaus took from him.

MAKE THE PUTT

When you are nervous over a putt, try to make it.

RAY WATSON

How about a little golfing advice from Shakespeare? This from that scratch golfer Hamlet:

Thus conscience does make cowards of us all,
And thus the native hue of resolution
Is sicklied o'er with the pale cast of thought.

Awareness of death, mortality, the afterlife makes us fearful, tainting our natural resolve.

Watson talks a lot about fear in golf. He thinks it deadens the nerves. It makes a golfer lose feeling in his hands and weakens his sense of moderation. In a phrase, it makes golfers sicklied o'er with the pale cast of thought. This is why Watson and Nicklaus and probably your local golf pro will tell you that when the pressure is at its highest and your adrenaline is pumping, you should take a little bit less club and swing fully.

In other words, if you are debating between a 7- and an 8-iron on an important shot, you should probably choose the 8-iron. When the pressure is hottest, touch is the first thing to go. Your best bet is to give yourself a full swing because your emotions are already so close to the surface.

Watson's father felt the same way about putting. Tom did not become golf's most aggressive putter by accident. Ray instilled that in his son. The thing about putting, Ray would say, is confidence. Belief. You can't make a putt if you leave it short. You can't be a good putter when you are defensive. Tom could not even count how many times in his young life he would leave a putt short only to hear his father say, "That was a terrible putt. You can't make a putt that doesn't reach the hole."

When the pressure is at its highest, golfers often leave putts short. Negative thoughts amplify under pressure. Negative thoughts lead to defensive maneuvers. Defensive maneuvers lead to leaving putts short.

Watson remembers standing over a putt he had on the 18th green at the 1977 Masters. He was two shots ahead of Nicklaus, so the championship seemed secure, but he knew that he shouldn't think that way. Instead he heard his father's voice. "I got a little nervous on the putt. All I needed to do was three-putt from thirty feet, but I had to stop thinking like that. Try to make it. That's what Dad always said. So I went back to the old school and tried to make it."

Watson left his first putt cozied up to the hole, he made his par, and he beat Nicklaus for the first time. "Sometimes I was too aggressive when trying to make putts. But Dad was right. Being too aggressive on putts will not hurt you as much as being too passive."

HOLE NO. 13

Watson went to Pebble Beach in 1982 feeling desperate. He still had not won the U.S. Open, the tournament that mattered most to him and to his father. He remembered the U.S. Open games they had played together, Ray barking out a year, Tom coming up with the winner and the golf course where it was played.

"Okay, smart guy, how about 1928?" Ray would ask.

"Tommy Armour at Oakmont," Tom would answer.

"No. That's 1927."

"Johnny Farrell."

"Right. But where did he win it?"

"Inverness?"

"Olympia Fields. You stink at this."

"Give me another one. I bet I'll get it."

They played this game so often that, long after he became an adult, Watson still remembered all the U.S. Open winners. He badly wanted his own year. And in 1982, going into Pebble Beach, he knew he wasn't playing well enough to win.

•   •   •

What was it about Nicklaus that brought out the best in Watson? Going into the 1981 Masters, Watson was playing mediocre golf. He had not won a tournament all year, and he actually missed the cut at the Tournament Players Championship, in which he had finished in the top ten every previous year.

In the first round he shot a bland 71. The talk in Augusta that week was the new bent-grass greens that had been put in; golfers were struggling with them. Nicklaus had shot a 70 that he insisted would have been a 65 if he'd made any putts at all. On Friday he putted better and shot 65. Watson was four strokes back.

"I would get excited when I saw Jack on the leaderboard," Watson said. "I wanted to test myself against the best."

Their competition took flight in the third round. Nicklaus's game drifted; he hit a ball into Rae's Creek on the 12th hole, then hit anther one into the creek at the 13th. Watson birdied three straight holes and found himself in the lead by two. Nicklaus birdied the 15th and 16th, while Watson made a double bogey at the 17th. Watson led Nicklaus by a shot when the third day ended.

Nicklaus shot even par on the last day, a solid round. In effect, he was once again challenging Watson to keep it together and beat him. Watson admitted afterward that he felt as nervous that day as he ever had on a golf course. But by then he had learned how to feed off his nerves. At the 12th hole, he knocked in a wicked eight-foot putt for par. At the 13th, he hit the ball into the water but responded with what *Sports Illustrated*'s Dan Jenkins called "the niftiest pitch anyone ever hit over a creek and under the circumstances."

The 15th was probably the decisive hole. Watson hit a 4-wood over the water to set up a long eagle putt. He hit that putt too hard, and the ball rolled an uncomfortable distance past the hole.

The 15th and 16th greens are next to each other at Augusta—this is where Nicklaus and Weiskopf had their back-and-forth birdie confrontation in 1975—so Watson watched Nicklaus knock in his birdie to cut the lead to one shot. The cheers hit Watson the way the sun hits a flower. He perked up, walked over to his own birdie putt, and knocked it in to take a two-shot lead.

On the 17th, Watson hit into a greenside bunker. This was when the nerves hit him hardest, but, as he told reporters afterward, "I've played nervous before." He hit his bunker shot to four feet and made a classic "Watson par." On the 18th, with a two-shot lead in hand, he made a more conventional par and then raised his arms in triumph. Nicklaus had spurred him to victory one more time.

"It was beyond argument," Nicklaus would write of this scene in his autobiography, "that Thomas Sturges Watson had replaced Jack William Nicklaus as the man to beat."

Minutes after beating Nicklaus again and winning the Masters, however, Watson was already talking about how badly he wanted to win the next U.S. Open.

Watson kept many of his emotions hidden from the press and public, but he never could hide his desperation to win the U.S. Open. It had become an annual drama. He tried different techniques, different strategies, different training methods.

"Nothing would please me more than to win the Open," he told reporters one year. "It remains my number-one goal." Another year he said, "I don't think I can be considered one of the great players if I don't win the U.S. Open." When asked how he would feel if he never won an Open, he answered, "Do I think about it? You bet I do. I don't think it's any secret that it would be a terrible disappointment if I never won a U.S. Open."

At other times, he tried to downplay the whole thing. "It's not *that* big a deal," he told *The Washington Post*'s John Feinstein. To *The New York Times*'s Dave Anderson he said, "The Open means more to my family and friends than it means to me."

Whatever strategy he employed, the result seemed to be the same. His best shot to win the U.S. Open had been his first, back in 1974 at the Massacre at Winged Foot. He played well at Baltusrol in 1980, but that was the week Nicklaus decided to be young again. Other than that, he did not threaten to win, and though he sometimes protested, it haunted him.

"Yes, I put more pressure on myself to win the U.S. Open," he admitted years later. "It's our national championship. It's the most important tournament in the world to me as an American. . . . All the greatest American golfers, with the exception of Sam Snead and now Phil Mickelson, won a U.S. Open. I wanted to be in their company."

In 1982 there was a new twist to the story: the tournament was at his beloved Pebble Beach. While at Stanford he had played Pebble Beach every Saturday. His favorite game there was something he called "Three pars to win the U.S. Open." He pretended that he needed pars on each of the closing three holes to win the U.S. Open. Whenever he failed—"I don't think I ever did make three pars in college"—he chastised himself, "You've got a long way to go."

Watson played imaginary U.S. Open games long after he graduated college. Byron Nelson watched him practice on the driving range, and every now and again he would hear Watson say something like "That's a perfect drive for number twelve at Pebble for the Open."

"It's there in his mind all the time," Nelson said.

•　　•　　•

Watson loved Pebble Beach utterly and completely, but the golf course loved Jack Nicklaus. There are, in sports, grand love affairs between athletes and their amphitheaters, between Roger Federer and the grass courts of Wimbledon, between Babe Ruth and Yankee Stadium, and so it was between Nicklaus and Pebble Beach. He won one of his two U.S. Amateurs there and won the Bing Crosby National Pro-Am there three times. He also won the first U.S. Open ever held at Pebble Beach, in 1972; he clinched that victory with one of golf's most famous shots, a 1-iron on the 17th that bounced, hit the flagstick, and dropped happily next to the hole.

"Why do you have so much success at Pebble Beach?" a reporter asked him before the 1982 U.S. Open.

"Because I shoot low scores," Nicklaus replied impatiently. He was not at Pebble Beach to suffer fools or to talk about the past. He was forty-two years old and he knew that he would not have many more chances. He was at Pebble Beach to win another U.S. Open. And he felt pretty sure that he would.

Watson felt lousy about his swing. Again. For three years he had felt focused, tuned, in control. He had felt so good about his game that he'd even shortened his practice schedule. He talked with Byron Nelson about it; Nelson had long wished for Watson to stop practicing so much, to realize that he'd reached a good place. He again told Watson the story of Ben Hogan saying that Nelson would be a lot better player if he practiced, when Nelson cheekily replied that he already had learned how to swing the golf club.

"Byron said it with a chuckle," Watson recalled. "But it was actually the truth. Byron had his 'Aha' moment at a young age and it stayed with him the rest of his life. The game is such a joy to play when you have control of your swing."

For those three years Watson had control. But something was changing in the weeks before Pebble Beach. His body was changing, and his swing was beginning to betray him again. "I've struggled, had to play defensively," he said at the time. When he got to Pebble Beach, matters got worse. He played dreadfully during his practice rounds. He hit the ball sideways. His caddie Bruce Edwards would remember seeing him looking ashen afterward.

"I didn't give myself one chance in a million to win the tournament," Watson said.

And for two rounds, he played just like he had practiced. He bogeyed the first three holes of the tournament and looked lost. He hit shots all over the place. With his swing untrustworthy, he had to revert to the college version of himself. He had to scramble. He had to make Watson pars. When the day ended, he was not just happy with the even-par score he managed; he was pretty well shocked by it. It had taken all the magic he had stored up. "I felt kind of like the fighters in Vegas," he told reporters. "I took some punches."

The second day, Watson hit the ball even worse. Again he reached into his past and made remarkable recovery shots and long putts. This was how he had played Pebble Beach on those Saturdays when he showed up at first light and they let him play for free. He somehow managed another even-par round. "I got away with murder out there," he said.

Watson was playing terribly, but somehow he was only five shots off the lead. He was tied with Nicklaus.

After the second round, Watson knew he could not win the golf tournament hitting the ball that way. He took a bucket of balls and went back to the practice range with Edwards and thought hard: What the heck was he doing wrong?

He went over all the usual suspects. Was he moving his head? No. Was he rushing through his backswing? Not really. How was his alignment? It seemed okay. How about the position of his hands at the top of his swing? No, that seemed good enough.

What was it? Watson hit a golf ball and pondered as the ball glided off-line. He tried something different. Same problem. He tried something else. No better. You know that feeling when you can't find your keys? You know they are around somewhere, probably closer than you think, but you just can't find them. Watson hit another ball, then another, then another, none of them feeling right.

And then he hit a shot and something felt different. What was that? He put another ball down, hit it, and yes, something definitely felt different. He looked down as he practiced it again. What was he doing differently? He suspected that he was keeping his left arm closer to his body as he turned on the backswing. Could it be that simple? Could it be that he had been letting his left arm get too far away? He put down a golf ball and swung with that one thought: Keep your left arm in. The ball soared majestically.

He hit another ball: Keep your left arm in. The ball again flew straight.

"Bruce," he said to his caddie, "I got it."

PLAY WITH PURPOSE

Jack practiced better than anybody. He didn't waste a single shot. There was always a purpose for every shot he hit.

TOM WATSON

Weekend golfers generally don't like to practice. There is so little time for golf in our lives; when a slot does open up, who wants to spend it hitting golf balls on a driving range or working on shots out of the sand? Watson believes, though, that a few minutes of practice can change a golfer's life. It just has to be the right kind of practice.

The right kind of practice, he says, is the Jack Nicklaus kind of practice. Watson is quick to say that he himself was not as disciplined a practice player as Nicklaus. Watson was renowned for how hard he worked on the practice range, for the time he spent out there, and it is true that nobody put in more time or had greater dedication. His teacher Stan Thirsk said Watson got tendinitis as a kid from hitting too many golf balls off the frozen Kansas City ground. But Watson says his kind of unrelenting practice is not the right kind of practice for most people.

"I just went out and hit balls," he explains. "I hit sometimes in anger because I had a bad round. I hit sometimes in frustration. I hit sometimes because I just liked practice. I wanted to go out there and hit good shot after good shot after good shot, and that is probably the wrong thing to do. You get to a certain point where you will hit a good shot, but you won't figure out exactly how you hit that good shot.

"Other times you go out and hit a series of good shots and maybe a few bad or questionable shots. Still you hit a lot of good shots. But that wasn't enough for me. I wanted to hit them *all* good. So I continued to practice. Rarely did I get to the point where I thought, 'Yeah, I got it. Every shot is good.'"

Watson insists you should emulate the way Nicklaus practices. Yes, Nicklaus too worked long hours, especially as a young man building his game. But for most of his career, he did not put in the hours that Watson did. Nicklaus says plainly, "I really didn't work all that hard at the game in some of my best years."

"What Jack did," Watson says, "was concentrate on each shot. He might only be out there for fifteen minutes, but he had a purpose for every one of those fifteen minutes. He was working on something. I see golfers go out to the range and just hit balls carelessly. That's not helpful. In fact, it's probably hurting you because it is ingraining bad habits."

The secret, then, is to think through practice shots, hit each one with a certain purpose. Then carry over this mental discipline to the golf course. So many golfers flail and never even consider why. There's a story about a golf instructor seeing a golfer on a practice range hit wild slice after wild slice. Finally, after watching the man hit ten terrible shots in a row without pausing even for a moment between them, the instructor walked over and asked, "Why do you think you're slicing the ball so much?"

The man shook his head. "I have no idea."

"Well then," the instructor said, "keep at it. You should have that slice down by the end of the day."

HOLE NO. 14

This is the magic of golf. One day, everything fails: drives spin out of control; balls nestle deep into the rough; putts lip out; your golf swing feels heavy and out of control. Then, the very next day, all of it turns. As he began the third round of the U.S. Open, Watson's swing felt right, and he knew that he would play well.

Saturday at Pebble Beach was cool and damp—"It's like a British course with the sea and the cold weather," Watson said—and his swing felt breezy. He shot a 4-under 68 to tie Bill Rogers for the lead. "I love the way I'm swinging the club," he told reporters after that third round. "I can't wait for tomorrow."

Nicklaus too loved the way he was swinging the club, but his putting was killing him. Time and again he missed birdie chances. He ended Saturday trailing Watson and Rogers by three shots. If he had putted well, he thought, he would be leading by five.

"No, I'm not upset about my putting," he said after the round, sarcasm dripping off each word. "These greens at Pebble Beach are hard to read. I've only been playing them for 21 years. One of these years I'll figure them out."

Nicklaus still felt sure that he was going to win. How? He'd find a way. The writer Dan Jenkins's line on Nicklaus described him perfectly: "It was almost as if he felt it was his birthright to win majors." Nicklaus had a Trojan's sense of destiny. "I'm due to make some putts," he told reporters. And then, somewhat ominously, he reminded everyone, "I've been through this before."

For years, Nicklaus, like Watson, had stayed with the same caddie, Angelo Argea, a big Greek with a gray Afro. Argea was as much a bodyguard as a caddie for Nicklaus. His main job was not to read greens, suggest clubs, or step off yardage; Nicklaus generally was his own counsel. When Argea was asked what he did for Nicklaus, he explained that he did three things:

1. He carried the bag.
2. He reminded Nicklaus occasionally that he was the best golfer in the world.
3. When the time was right, he would say something like "There are a lot of holes left."

This was exactly what Nicklaus needed in his prime. Argea was his version of the slaves who walked behind great Roman warriors and whispered, "Fame is fleeting." Nicklaus and Argea worked together until the late 1970s. Then Argea wrote a book called *The Bear and I*. Nicklaus didn't mind that he wrote the book, and he did not mind what was written in it. But he did mind that one year at Pinehurst, Argea was so distracted promoting the book that he did not go out on the course and get the exact pin placements of a couple of holes.

"I said to him, 'Angelo, you didn't get this, did you?'" Nicklaus recalls. "He said, 'No, boss, I got tied up.' So I just said to him,

'Angelo, you've caddied for me for, gracious, twenty-five years. I think it's time we part as friends."

So it was not Argea on the bag at Pebble Beach that Sunday when Nicklaus trailed by four shots while playing the third hole. Nicklaus had hit his approach shot fifteen feet from the hole, the putting distance that had bedeviled him for three days. Then his caddie said something inspirational: "This is where the U.S. Open begins."

Nicklaus smiled and promptly knocked in the putt. He turned to catch the eye of his caddie, Jackie Nicklaus, his twenty-year-old son. Yes, Jack Nicklaus felt the brilliance of the moment. He was with his son. It was Father's Day. And the U.S. Open was beginning.

At the 4th hole, Nicklaus made a twenty-five-foot putt for birdie and raised his putter to the sky. The 5th hole at Pebble Beach is a tricky par 3; Nicklaus hit his tee shot pure, and the ball stopped two feet left of the hole. He looked over at Jackie and rolled his eyes. That birdie putt put him one shot behind Watson.

On the par-5 6th hole, Nicklaus smashed a 1-iron shot onto the green in two and made his fourth straight birdie. Then, at the 7th hole, a beautiful little par 3 that overlooks the ocean, his ball rolled to within ten feet of the hole. The putt curled left to right, dropped in, and once more Nicklaus raised his putter high. Less than an hour after his son said the U.S. Open had begun, Nicklaus led the tournament.

When reporters asked Watson why he had never won the U.S. Open, he struggled for a reason. "I really can't put my finger on why I haven't been able to do it." Then he added, "I'm going to try my damnedest to win tomorrow. But if I don't, there's always next year."

Deep down Watson knew: there was no next year. No, it had to be this year. He was almost thirty-three, and he already sensed his game drifting. And this U.S. Open was at Pebble Beach, *his* Pebble Beach. He had invested too many of his dreams in this place. It had to be this year. When Sunday came, he felt calm and confident—until he started hearing the roars. At first they sounded like distant thunder, just rumbles, but they grew louder as the afternoon went on. Those cheers, he knew, could be for only one man. Nicklaus, it seemed, had taken flight.

Watson came to the 7th hole trailing by one stroke, and he hit perhaps his best shot of the day, a crisp 9-iron that stopped eighteen inches from the hole. That birdie would tie him with Nicklaus—but he missed it. He hit the ball too hard and didn't read enough left-to-right break; the ball skimmed the left side of the cup and spun away. Golfers who miss eighteen-inch putts do not win the U.S. Open.

This, though, is where Watson's greatest attribute shone through. If Nicklaus won tournaments by embracing a grand destiny, Watson won by refusing to accept a doomed fate. No golfer before or since moved on from a bad shot quite like Tom Watson.

"I just keep going back to this," Gary Koch said. "Tom played the game the way you play it as a kid. He just loved being out there. He just wanted a chance to play the next shot. When I got into professional golf, it was more like a business. It was my job, how I make a living, how I feed my family. I probably lost some of that childlike wonder about the game. But Tom—I never saw Tom lose it. He just had this amazing ability to deal with less than ideal shots. That was the kid in him. He just shook it off, 'No big deal, I'll get the next one.' It's something every golfer strives for, but for Tom it was natural."

Watson concurred: "Of course I wasn't happy when I missed

that putt at the seventh. But it was a tricky putt and, anyway, after I missed, it was over. I was a shot back at the U.S. Open. It was just where I wanted to be. I wasn't going to win the U.S. Open by worrying about a missed putt."

Nicklaus had more success at Pebble Beach than anyone. Here was his theory of how to win there: "Beat up the first seven holes then hang on for dear life." He had followed his plan perfectly. He had made five birdies in the first seven holes and, with the U.S. Open lead in hand, moved on to the hang-on-for-dear-life portion of the golf course.

Watson had played uninspired golf the first seven holes. He shot 1-over par on the front nine and promptly got himself into a mess on the 10th hole, hitting his approach shot into the rough. When he got to the ball, he saw that it was on a downslope and there was no chance to get the ball close to the hole. He chipped out a shot to twenty-five feet, the best he could do, and then braced himself while golf analysts talked about how difficult it would be to two-putt the hole for bogey.

Then Watson did what he so often did: he made the absurd putt for par.

He faced an even grislier putt at the 14th hole, this one from thirty-five feet away. Dan Jenkins saw the putt and was not sure it was even geometrically possible to get the ball close to the hole. Watson's playing partner Bill Rogers agreed: "That's a place where humans three-putt from."

Watson made the putt and took the U.S. Open lead from Nicklaus.

"Why not?" Jenkins wrote. "Watson is as good a putter as there is in the game today, and perhaps the finest long-putter, period. He has been sinking putts like that one for seven years."

Nicklaus was in the clubhouse at 4-under par when Watson came to the 16th hole leading by a shot. Here was the game he used to play back in college come to life: he needed three pars to win the U.S. Open. But he did not make even one. He floundered on the 16th hole. His drive dropped into a new fairway bunker (one recommended by his friend Sandy Tatum). The ball was buried deep enough that Watson had to hit out sideways. His third shot was, in his own words, lousy and rolled to the back of the green. It was such a treacherous putt that even the bold Watson could not try to make it; he tried instead to hit the ball close enough so that he'd have a good look at bogey and could go to the 17th tied for the lead.

"I hit my best putt of the day there," Watson would say. "It broke about ten feet and it ended up a couple of feet from the hole. That was the best I could do. I was tied with Jack."

The 17th at Pebble Beach is a beautiful and ill-natured par 3 by the sea. The hole is more than two hundred yards long with an hourglass-shaped green. The wind always blows. If you hit the ball long, it's dead; the ocean is back there. If you hit the ball left, it's dead; there's a huge bunker there and high rough. If you hit the ball right, it's dead: more bunkers and rough.

Still, with a perfect shot at number 17 comes glory. It was here that Nicklaus hit the 1-iron that bounced off the flagstick and won him the 1972 U.S. Open. A shot like that could win Watson the Open ten years later.

Watson stepped to the tee. How did he feel? Calm, he remembers. He was no longer the kid who choked, and he was no longer the young man who questioned his own talent. He was, plainly, the best golfer in the world. He held his 2-iron, and he knew exactly what he had to do. He swung, and he hit the ball solidly. He watched the ball soar. And then he watched the ball turn left. He had hooked it, and the ball flew long and left and buried deep into the Pebble Beach rough. "Well, that's dead," he said to Edwards. Another heart was broken at 17.

Nicklaus walked off the 18th green believing that he had won the U.S. Open, and he happily tossed his ball into the crowd. His logic was simple: Watson needed to par the last two holes just to force a playoff. That was a brutal task even under the tamest conditions, and these were not tame conditions. Nicklaus knew how badly Watson wanted this U.S. Open, how much pressure he would be feeling.

While being interviewed by ABC's Jack Whitaker, he saw Watson hook his shot to the left at No. 17. Dead. Nicklaus knew that Watson had a miraculous short game, but the shot he would face was beyond even his magnificent gifts. A bogey was all but assured. He felt a pang of disappointment for his friend, but damn it, that guy had taken enough tournaments away from him. Nicklaus was going to win the U.S. Open.

Bruce Edwards had watched Watson rebound from bad shots again and again through the years. How many times had Edwards felt discouraged only to see Watson make some supernatural shot from an impossible place? Dead? No. Watson was never dead.

"Come on!" Edwards urged as they began their walk to the ball. "Let's get it up and down."

Watson nodded, smiled that mysterious smile, and sure enough, his first reaction when he saw his ball in the rough was something like "Hey, wait, that's not too bad." The ball was visible. Sure, he was facing an absurdly hard shot: ball in tall grass, downhill lie, downhill green, no room to maneuver, no chance to stop the ball. But an absurdly hard shot is not the same thing as an impossible shot.

And there was another thing: he had practiced this shot. He had practiced it perhaps more than any human being in the world. Just that week he had taken extra time to practice these sorts of delicate chip shots. "I was hitting the ball so cruddy," he said, "that I figured I better practice shots around the greens."

All his life Watson was drawn to these kinds of preposterous shots. They were like little magic tricks. "Let me tell you what still thrills me," he says many years after Pebble Beach. "It thrills me to hit shots that people can admire and wonder, 'How the hell did he do that?'"

Watson looked at the ball, he looked at the hole, and he walked the distance between. The more he looked at it, the more he had this strange feeling.

"Get it close," Edwards told him.

"Get it close, hell," Watson said. "I'm going to make it."

Back at the clubhouse, Nicklaus was being congratulated on national television for winning the U.S. Open. This was how sure everyone was that Watson could not make his par. And maybe Nicklaus too got carried away by the moment. He might have remembered what happened to him at the Open Championship in 1972, when he made an extraordinary charge on the final day at Muirfield and seemed to have won while Lee Trevino faced a seemingly impossible chip on the 17th hole. Nicklaus would tell the story this way: "Trevino hit [a] give-up chip. He didn't think he had any chance to get the ball close." The ball went in the hole anyway and Trevino won.

Yes, Nicklaus knew what was possible. Still, he stood there

happily as Jack Whitaker said, "Congratulations on winning your fifth Open. It has been an honor covering golf in your time."

In Nicklaus's memory, it was just when Whitaker said the words "your time" that he heard the impossibly loud roar of the crowd.

Watson kept thinking about one word, *soft*, as he hit the chip. He needed the ball to pop out soft and fluffy, like dandelion seeds, because anything carrying speed would roll way past the hole. Sure enough, he hit it soft. The rest was up to the Fates. He watched as the ball landed on the green, began rolling, and then, as he hoped, started breaking left toward the flag. It was rolling fast, but there was nothing he could do about that. He just hoped that it would hit the flagstick and stop.

The ball hit the flagstick. And it dropped in.

"What can you say?" ABC's Jim McKay shouted. "Tom Watson pitching into the hole for a birdie has taken the lead of the U.S. Open."

Watson ran down to the green and kept running. He was so happy that his thoughts were little more than a jumble of exclamation marks. Then he stopped and turned and pointed at Edwards. "I told you!" he shouted.

At first Nicklaus didn't know what the roar meant. He asked someone, "What did he do, hit the pin?" When told that Watson had knocked it into the hole, Nicklaus would remember, he said just three words: "Aw, come on."

"Nicklaus is watching on our monitor," McKay told America. "He now knows that he can't do a thing. A man like Jack Nicklaus doesn't like to stand there helpless."

•   •   •

The funny part is that more than thirty years later, Nicklaus's most vivid memory of the U.S. Open is not of Watson making that chip. Sure, he remembers the chip, but mostly because people will not let him forget it. The chip would become a piece of golf history, perhaps the game's most famous single shot. But what Nicklaus remembers is that Watson still needed to par the 18th hole to win.

Nicklaus had just played the par-5 18th hole and knew how difficult it was. He had a three-foot putt for par, and with the greens chewed up and breathtakingly fast that three-foot putt took all the nerve he had. He knew the U.S. Open was not over quite yet.

Watson played a 3-wood off the tee, laid up his second shot in the fairway, and hit a wonderful approach to about twenty-five feet from the hole. His putt was downhill all the way, and if he hit it too hard he could face a difficult par putt coming back. He hit it too hard anyway.

"It was going twenty miles per hour," Nicklaus said. "I remember thinking, 'It's going to go seven or eight feet by. He is going to have a putt like that to win the U.S. Open.'"

But the ball didn't roll by the hole. It dived into the cup. Watson had won.

The first thing he did was call his father at home in Kansas City.

"Why the hell didn't you lag that putt?" Ray scolded.

"It went in, didn't it? Happy Father's Day."

Neither man remembers exactly what Nicklaus said to Watson as they embraced after the U.S. Open. Dan Jenkins and others reported Nicklaus saying, "You little son of a bitch, you're something else." Nicklaus remembered it as "You little S.O.B., I'm going to get you someday." Watson recalled it like so: "You little son of a bitch, you did it to me again. I'm proud of you."

But both remember what happened later. They were alone. Something had changed between them. Nicklaus was forty-two and beginning to see the end. Watson was thirty-two and closer to the end than he could have known. They both knew that there might not be another grand duel.

"Jack," Watson said, "you're the greatest player in our game's history."

"Tom," Nicklaus said, "you needed to win. You needed to win that U.S. Open."

EXPECT BAD SHOTS

Even the best golfers in the world hit bad shots. Golf is a hard game. I think people sometimes forget that. I will hear amateur golfers saying to themselves, "Why can't I hit the ball straight?" I'll tell you why. Golf is a hard game. Give yourself a break.

TOM WATSON

As amateur athletes we have a tendency to visualize ourselves at our best. As tennis players we remember the aces and not the double faults. As bowlers we think of the split we once converted and not the easy spares we've missed. As baseball players, we think of the home runs and the great catches and leave behind the strikeouts and the balls that rolled through our legs.

This tendency is particularly true of golf. When a high-handicap golfer hits a wonderful shot exactly as planned, the feeling tends not to be "Wow, it's strange that a golfer of my meager ability would hit such a good shot." It leans instead toward "Yes, that's my game. That is who I am." The next twenty terrible shots are mere illusions until, finally, another good shot reminds the golfer of his true self.

This theme amuses Watson. He sees golfers slamming down

their clubs after hitting shots that are perfectly acceptable for players of their level. "You can fool yourself into thinking you are better than you are," he says. "And that actually can work sometimes. But you can also fool yourself into thinking you are worse than you are, and that's a negative. In the end, I think you have to be brutally honest with yourself and your assessment of how you're playing."

Before hitting every shot, Watson insists that you should imagine a good shot, even a perfect shot. There should be no negativity. When Watson said to Edwards at Pebble Beach, "Get it close, hell. I'm going to make it," he was only putting into words the image he visualized.

But visualization is one thing. Being brutally honest means expecting bad shots. Because the reality is you will hit a lot of bad shots. The secret is to move on from those bad shots, and the way to do that is to be ready for them. Watson was at heart a perfectionist, but nobody dealt with bad shots better than he did.

"I like what Ben Hogan said," Watson says. "He would ask, 'Why can't I birdie every hole on the golf course? Why can't I birdie all eighteen holes?' That's the eternal question of golf. It's the thing you always try to do. And yet, it hasn't been done. Why? Because it's hard to be that exact. It's a hard game.

"You want to limit your bad shots, of course. But you will hit some bad ones. You have to expect that. If you expect bad shots, you can let go of them and get on with business."

HOLE NO. 15

Watson's slump began so quietly that just about the only person who noticed was Watson himself. One month after he won the U.S. Open, he won his fourth Open Championship. A year later, at Royal Birkdale in England, he won his fifth Open Championship. No American, not even Nicklaus, had done that.

That fifth Open Championship gave him eight total major championships, one more than his hero Arnold Palmer and one more than his father's hero Sam Snead. In the great major championship race, Watson trailed only Nicklaus, Walter Hagen, Ben Hogan, and Gary Player. He was still only thirty-four years old. People expected him to keep winning major championships for several more years.

But Watson wasn't so sure. People thought he was just being his typically overbearing self when he grumbled that he did not feel good about his game. Even friends sighed and shook their heads when he began tinkering with his swing again. They couldn't see what he could see: his game was eroding, as was his confidence. The Open Championship in 1983 was his only victory that year. He began 1984 by missing three cuts in a row. In Hawaii he uncharacteristically lost his cool and screamed at Edwards over a misunderstanding; it was the first time Edwards had seen Watson lose his temper on the golf course. "You could see it coming," Edwards told John Garrity of *Sports Illustrated*. He meant the slump.

Watson still had good moments. He finished second at the Masters to Ben Crenshaw. He was tied for the lead at the Open Championship at St. Andrews on the final day when he made bogey on the famous road hole. ("The old lady got me," he told reporters.) He won three times in 1984 and, for the fifth time in his career, led the PGA Tour in earnings. He was named PGA Tour Player of the Year for the sixth time.

Still, Watson knew. The slump had begun.

Golf can be a cruel game. Watson's swing began to betray him the year he turned thirty-five. This can happen to even the greatest golfers. There are so many elements in a golf swing, and when one goes even slightly wrong—one degree too steep, one millimeter too far left or right, one notch too low or high—the whole swing can fall apart.

Then the golfer must try to find the flaw by going through a checklist roughly the length of the one used for Apollo 13: recheck the grip, the alignment, the angle of the takeaway, head placement, head movement, the arc of the swing, the depth of the swing, the placement of hands at impact, the fullness of the follow-through, and so on. There's no guarantee that you will ever find the problem.

Watson did not win a tournament in 1985 or 1986, mostly because he could not find the flaw in his swing. Every now and again, he talked about making progress. He talked about an approaching breakthrough. He finally won a tournament in 1987, and there were a few "Tom is back" stories. But they were wrong.

Instead Watson's game went off the rails. In 1988 he had only one top-five finish. The next year he missed five cuts. Golf can be a cruel game. While Watson's swing problems had started the slump, it was something else that brought his game to its knees. The most aggressive and successful putter of his generation stopped making putts.

He also started drinking heavily.

Nicklaus and Watson had become close friends in the years after their duels. When Watson's game went south, Nicklaus offered a few bits of advice. When Nicklaus won his last great tournament, the 1986 Masters, Watson said that it was as if he himself had won. They played practice rounds together. They played in team competitions together. They went to dinner together and argued politics. Nicklaus, though moderately conservative, generally found himself miles to the left of Watson.

But to Nicklaus, Watson always kept some part of himself to himself, distant. Nicklaus wrote in his autobiography, "What became apparent as we spent increasing time together on and off the course is that all-around buddyism just isn't his style. Many of our mutual acquaintances have found Tom hard to get to know as a man, and that includes a large percentage of tour players from the best to the also-rans. There is a depth of reserve there that creates a shell that is difficult to penetrate. You can be talking to Tom and have the sense that, although he's listening on the surface, on the inside he's not really with you."

Watson agrees with Nicklaus's assessment. He had no talent, nor any interest, in "all-around buddyism." He played golf to win, and he kept his home life private. He often preferred to be alone. In the best of times, he seemed uncomfortable to people around him. When his game went bad, everything went bad. Even two decades later, he did not want to talk about those trying years. He would only say, "It hurt every single part of my life." Then he paused. "I hated the game. I really hated it."

"Did you ever think of quitting golf?" I asked him.

"I hated it. Don't you understand? There's nothing else that needs to be said."

"Did you ever think of quitting?"

"No."

People around America sent him putters; for a time his office in Kansas City had a hundred different putters leaning up against the walls. They were only trying to help. Some sent him putting advice: Putt with one eye closed, cross-handed, with one hand, left-handed, on one leg. And some sent him putting gadgets. They sent him elixirs to calm his nerves, good luck charms to change his fortunes, mantras to chant.

He could not explain what it felt like to lose his putting touch. Putting had been his superpower. He had always made putts.

"Tom was fearless," Nicklaus would say. "He putted fearlessly. That's a very rare thing. There were times, I think, I was too tentative a putter. I think most golfers would tell you that. But not Tom. He wanted to make everything. For a long time he did."

Why did Watson stop making putts? Well, age does prey on a golfer's putting. At the end Ben Hogan would sometimes freeze when standing over a putt, as if he was afraid of making a stroke. "Putting is not golf," Hogan would grumble, and it was a sentiment many great golfers felt as they grew older.

"God only gives you so many nerve endings to burn up through pressure," Watson said of putting. "And when you burn through them, you can't get them back."

The other great golfers who lost their putting strokes—Hogan, Sam Snead, Johnny Miller—were not great putters as young men. But it was different for Watson. He *was* great. And it left so suddenly.

When Watson himself speaks about it, he speaks philosophically: "You can only make so many putts in your life. I just happened to make mine when I was young."

Friends and competitors blame Watson's drinking. When he stopped winning, he drank more. "He never seemed to enjoy drinking," one friend says. "He would just have one glass of wine after another. He wasn't very happy then."

"Why did Tom stop making putts?" another friend asks, and, as an answer, he lifts an invisible glass to his lips. "Nobody in the world putted like Tom when he was young. Nobody. I think the drinking rattled his nerves. That's what alcohol does."

A life is rarely simple, and big questions rarely have one answer. Did Watson drink too much because he missed putts? Did he miss putts because he drank too much? The record shows that for the decade after he won the 1984 Open Championship, he won just one tournament, and he missed a million putts. Watson admits that he drank too much. Did it affect his game? He will say only that he was miserable.

The story of Nicklaus winning the Masters in 1986, when he was forty-six, has become golf legend. Nicklaus was no longer a great player. He had won just one tournament in four years. His life had shifted away from playing. He was spending more time with his businesses and his family. And then he had a week that played out like a made-for-television movie.

Early in the week, a reporter for an Atlanta newspaper wrote a story calling Nicklaus washed up. As a gag, a friend of

Nicklaus stuck the clipping on the refrigerator, where he was sure not to miss it. Nicklaus read it again and again as the week went on.

Nicklaus always seemed to know what score he needed to shoot to win, and that Sunday morning before the final round he calculated that he needed a 7-under par 65. He was even par through the first eight holes. Then, on the last ten, the years melted away. He made a downhill putt at the 9th for birdie. "Here we go," he remembers thinking.

He made a twenty-five-foot putt for birdie at the 10th and a twenty-footer for birdie at the 11th. The leaders were a charismatic Spaniard named Seve Ballesteros and the young Australian Greg Norman. But the galleries seemed to leave them when Nicklaus birdied the 13th hole. When he got to the par-5 15th, he turned to his son and caddy Jackie and asked, "How far do you think a three would go here?"

"Pretty far," Jackie answered. "Let's see it."

Nicklaus hit a magnificent 4-iron, and the ball settled twelve feet from the cup. When he knocked it in, the roars rattled through the trees. On the 16th tee, he pulled out a 5-iron and carefully studied the shot. He seemed to take forever before hitting; he knew how to disappear into himself in the biggest moments. Then the ball soared right for the flag.

"Be the right club!" Jackie shouted in prayer, and his dad looked back and winked.

"It is."

The ball stopped three feet from the hole. Nicklaus made birdie there and faced a tricky eighteen-foot putt on the next hole. The putt was what is called a double breaker, meaning it would break left and then right. Nicklaus made that putt too. He had the lead at the Masters. At the 18th hole, he was careful not to make the misjudgment he had made in 1977 when facing Watson. He played conservatively, made his par, and won his sixth Masters.

"He had told everybody, 'I didn't expect to win,'" Watson would say. "It was such a Nicklausian comment. He said, 'I didn't expect to win. This is a tournament for young people. Young nerves.' But he never stopped expecting to win. Not Jack.

"I remember him hugging Jackie, and that was so awesome. That's the memory I keep. Jack deserved one more moment like that for all he had done for the game."

FOLLOW THE FEELING

I always tell people that you want to hold the club firmly, but you don't want to squeeze it. That's the proper pressure—hold it firmly but don't squeeze.

TOM WATSON

Golf lessons often exasperate. Sensible golf tips found in a golf magazine sometimes lead to frustration. When John Updike's golf game withered, he wrote in "Golf Dreams," he found himself staring helplessly at a list of tips he had jotted down that once meant something to him but now seemed as nonsensical as snippets of old nursery rhymes.

1. Loose grip. . . .
7. Don't try to "swish." . . .
9. Think "schwooo."

There are basics of golf that work, basics about how to grip the club, how far to stand from the ball, how to align yourself, how to pull the club back, how to follow through. And knowing those basics is the foundation of a good swing. But any golfer understands that some parts of the game are not knowable. Some parts of the swing are felt and not entirely understood.

Watson has probably spent as much time as anyone considering the technical aspects of the golf swing. But even he says there are things you cannot communicate. What, after all, does "Hold the club firmly but don't squeeze" even mean? To squeeze, according to the Cambridge Dictionary, means "to press something firmly." How can you hold the club firmly without squeezing it?

"That's what a golfer has to figure out," Watson says. "And it's a constant struggle. For me, it comes from hitting a million golf balls. You achieve an understanding of what works and what doesn't work in certain situations. And if you have a good enough memory, you can bank on those experiences with those memories to help you out when you're struggling with a particular shot or a particular swing."

Those memories, he says, are of feelings. So Updike's tips are not nonsensical at all; "Think 'schwooo'" was his personal way of trying to capture how it felt when he hit a golf ball crisply. Feeling is what Watson believes is at the crux of golf. You want to follow tips so that you can hit good shots. But more than that, you want to remember how it *feels* to hit a good shot.

Then you want to chase that feeling.

HOLE NO. 16

Watson remembers the exact time and place when he found the Secret. It was April 14, 1994, right at 3:15 p.m. on a Tuesday afternoon in Hilton Head, South Carolina. He had finished out of the top ten at the Masters again, for the third year in a row at a tournament where he had been a perennial contender, and he was miserable. The slump had overwhelmed everything in his life. His shots sliced right. His putts lipped out. He was so frustrated that he more or less stopped practicing. He cut his tournament schedule. He was unhappy. When Bruce Edwards was offered a chance to become the regular caddy for Greg Norman, then the No. 1 golf moneymaker in the world, Watson all but insisted that he take the job. "You have to do what's best for you, Bruce, not what's best for me," he told Edwards. When Edwards protested, Watson shook his head sadly. "I'm not playing well," he said, and then added plainly, "I don't know if I'll ever play well. This is still a business, Bruce. Do what's best for yourself."

Edwards could barely stand to see Watson like this. The man who used to wink after bad shots and say, "Watch what I do with this," now seemed resigned to bad shots. The man who used to slam putts at the hole with confidence now stood tentatively over easy short putts. The man who stood on the practice range for so many hours had mostly stopped practicing. Edwards did go to work for Norman. He wondered if his friend would ever break out of his funk.

That's what it was: a funk. Watson hated golf. It was the strangest feeling.

And then, at 3:15 p.m. on a Tuesday in Hilton Head, Watson was halfheartedly practicing for the Heritage Classic. And everything changed one more time.

In 1990, one of Watson's worst years on the Tour, the Kansas City Country Club refused membership to H&R Block's founder, Henry Bloch, because he was Jewish. Watson had managed for years to tune out the club's discriminatory policies even though his wife, Linda, was Jewish and they were raising their children Jewish. He had been raised at the Country Club. The place was his father's sanctuary. So Watson held his tongue.

But when the club blackballed Bloch, this crossed the line. Watson quit. All around the country, he was lauded for taking a stand—and the club did admit Bloch soon after—but Watson did not feel like his stand was something to celebrate. His quitting created a rift with his father that took years to mend. It put distance between him and all those Kansas City golfers, his heroes, who had pushed him and challenged him and inspired him to become the best golfer in the world. He did not want to quit. He had to quit.

The newspapers described Watson as principled. This was, perhaps, even truer than they realized. Watson's life overflowed with powerful principles, some that made sense to others and some, frankly, that did not. Nobody who knew him was surprised that he told Edwards to go caddy for Norman. Loyalty was one of Watson's most important principles.

Some of his other principles were harder to explain. When he became friends with Byron Nelson, one of the things he admired most was not Nelson's beautiful swing or his positive attitude; it was his view on dishwashers. "He and Louise, then Peggy, one would clean, the other would dry," Watson said. "They never used a dishwasher. I watched that."

Watson says he has never used a dishwasher. Not once. Why? It's a Tom Watson principle. To Watson, you clean dishes better by hand. To Watson, a dishwasher is simply a way to avoid honest work. To Watson, you build closer family relationships when everyone washes the dishes together.

Watson swore by what others might call old-fashioned values. He was a grammar scold; he did not hesitate to correct people around him, and every so often he would check himself to make sure he wasn't sliding into poor grammatical habits. He was a stickler for golf's rules, even wrote books about them—*The Rules of Golf, Illustrated and Explained* was the one of several—and these were labors of love. He griped to friends all the time that society was losing discipline—all that dishwasher use, perhaps—and was bending rules to the point of breaking. This is why he loved golf so much: even the most obscure and overly rigid rules were enforced fully. He did not like chipping away at the sanctity of golf.

That was a principle too: the sanctity of golf. In 1994 he wrote a letter to the Augusta National leadership asking them to remove the analyst Gary McCord from the CBS Masters television broadcast. McCord had built his reputation on being offbeat and a nonconformist. He had a handlebar mustache, excelled at close-up magic, and wrote down funny one-liners to use on the air. At Augusta he said the greens were so fast that they seemed bikini-waxed. Describing some hills off the greens, he said that was where the bodies were buried. Away from the golf community that sounded like G-rated silliness, jokes that would barely qualify as irreverent. In Watson's world, however, they were out of bounds. He wrote his letter, and Augusta National had Mc-Cord removed.

Two decades later, in 2014, Watson was named captain of the Ryder Cup team for the second time. The United States had not won a Ryder Cup on European soil in twenty-one years (not since the first time Watson was captain), and the PGA of America thought the team needed an infusion of Watson's passion and competitive fury.

It was a dreadful blend of personalities. The young golfers did not get Watson, and he did not get them. When the team struggled in the foursome competition, Watson reportedly told them, "You guys stink at foursomes." When the longtime star Phil Mickelson all but pleaded to be put into the afternoon competition on the second day, Watson told him no. When the team gave him a replica Ryder Cup trophy, he bruised feelings by saying the gift meant nothing to him.

Anyone who knew Watson—and you would have thought the PGA of America knew Watson—would have expected that. He was a man of blunt opinions. He was famously stubborn. No one who had spent any time with him would have thought it a good idea to give him a replica Ryder Cup on the night before the team was going to lose. But this was the gap between the captain and the players, and when the team did lose Mickelson sharply criticized Watson's captaining, and the PGA of America ran for the hills. Watson found himself apologizing and looking very much like a man out of time.

He was a man out of time.

"My father believed in old-fashioned values," Watson would say. "And we all end up like our parents."

Watson stood on the practice tee that day in Hilton Head in 1994 and tried something he had seen the golfer Corey Pavin do. Pavin was about Watson's height and body type, but unlike the aging Watson, he never seemed to miss a fairway. In his practice swings, he would make an exaggerated motion, taking the club way inside (close to his body) on the backswing and then moving it way outside (away from his body) on the downswing.

Watson that day tried to hit a golf ball using the Pavin swing. He pulled back on an exaggerated angle, came around in what seemed to him a crazy loop, and hit the ball. And he hit the ball perfectly.

He stared at the ball in flight. It was controlled, exactly where he aimed. He looked at his divot; he has long believed that the way to know if you hit a good shot is to look at the divot. He had been pulling toe-first divots out of the ground for years; these were odd-shaped divots caused when the toe of his club hit the ground first. But this divot was square. It was perfect. Watson quickly dropped another ball. He went through his Corey Pavin swing again and hit the ball.

And again he hit it perfectly.

One more time. He could feel his heart beating a little faster. He put the ball down and did the amplified swing one more time.

And one more time: perfect.

"Bruce," he said to Edwards, who had come back to be his caddie again, "I got it."

Watson, like Ben Hogan almost fifty years earlier, called his discovery "the Secret." It gave his game new life. It gave him new life. Watson was forty-four years old, he had not won a tournament in seven years, and he had all but given up on ever winning another one. Then he found his swing. He would never lose it again.

When Watson won again, Nicklaus waited for him at the 18th hole. That was at the 1996 Memorial Tournament, Nicklaus's home tournament in Columbus. Watson went into the final day with a lead and a sense of destiny. It had been nine years since he'd won a tournament. He had played well in the two years since he found the Secret—"I was hitting the ball as well as I ever had," he would say—but his putting never did come back. He gave himself chance after chance to win, but he could not.

That day in Columbus, he felt something different. Maybe it was Nicklaus's presence. Their friendship had evolved into something different from what either expected in the days when they competed for best in the world. They were both growing old, and it was not easy for either of them.

Nicklaus had always made it clear that he had no intention of becoming a ceremonial golfer like his friend and rival Arnold Palmer. Arnie never lost his joy for the game, even after he stopped winning. He would buddy up to sponsors and chat with people in the galleries and smile for anyone with a camera; he enjoyed that stuff. Nicklaus did not.

A reporter at the 1994 Masters started to say, "Jack, you have never missed a cut at the Masters and . . ."

"Really?" Nicklaus growled, interrupting. "That's where we are? That's what we're talking about? We're talking about making cuts now?" He was fifty-four years old but still sure of himself. "If I didn't think I could win, I wouldn't be here. I didn't come here to make the cut."

As it turns out, Nicklaus did not make the cut at the Masters that year, and later in the year he missed cuts at the Open Championship and the PGA Championship. His game was fading. It was something he could talk about with Watson. When Watson went into the last day of the Memorial with a lead, Nicklaus felt a few of his old competitive juices flowing. Watson faced an exacting four-foot putt early in the round, exactly the sort of putt that had tormented him for a decade.

"Come on, Tom," Nicklaus said quietly.

Watson knocked it in. He made a twenty-foot putt for birdie at the 13th. And, with a one-shot lead on the 18th green, he made a downhill twelve-footer to win by two.

Then Watson walked over to his old friend, who was standing on the fringe, and they embraced.

"I couldn't be happier for anyone," Nicklaus said. "I couldn't be happier."

"Thank you, my friend," Watson replied.

They saw each other more often as the years went along. Watson turned fifty and joined the Senior Tour. Nicklaus, who was already sixty, still played a few senior tournaments. They played Turnberry together as old men, at the 2003 Senior British Open. Reporters asked what they remembered most about the Duel in the Sun.

"I don't remember anything," Nicklaus said.

"That's what you keep on saying," responded Watson. "See, you lie like a rug."

At the time, the young Tiger Woods was dominating the game like no one, not even Nicklaus, ever had. Woods won four major championships in a row. He passed Watson on the PGA Tour victory list before he turned thirty and, not long after, passed Nicklaus too. No other golfer seemed able to challenge him. At

Turnberry, Nicklaus was asked if golf could use another rivalry like Nicklaus-Watson. He answered in Nicklaus understatement: "Couldn't hurt."

Woods was often the topic of discussion when Watson and Nicklaus got together. Both marveled at his brilliant game, his Watson-like hunger to win, his Nicklausian ability to conjure up a breathtaking shot at precisely the moment he needed it. After Nicklaus played a couple of rounds with the young Woods, he predicted Woods would "win more Masters than Arnold and me combined." (Palmer and Nicklaus won ten Masters between them.) When Watson was asked if Woods's great success would continue, he responded, "Well, he's the best driver of the ball, the best iron player, the best around the greens. He has the best imagination, he's in the best shape, he's the best pressure player, and he putts the ball better than anybody. So, yeah, I think he will probably keep winning."

Privately, though, they stewed about how other golfers capitulated to Woods's will. They seemed content to cash the enormous second- and third-place checks that Woods's popularity generated. Sometimes that private grumbling spilled into the media. In 2002 Watson invited Palmer, Player, Trevino, and Nicklaus to his annual Kansas City charity event supporting Children's Mercy Hospital. The group was asked if they would like to be younger so they could face Woods.

"You bet your ass I would," Palmer said.

"The golfers today give up," was Player's response.

Watson said, "I would love to try and beat that kid when I was a kid."

"Tiger has them all buffaloed," Nicklaus said, shaking his head. "If you don't believe you can win, you won't win. We believed."

• • •

There were tough times. Bruce Edwards, Watson's caddie and friend for the better part of thirty years, called him one day and said, "I made a quadruple bogey." This was his way of saying that he had been diagnosed with ALS.

"We'll beat it," Watson insisted, and for the next year they fought the disease together. Edwards carried Watson's bag for as long as he had the strength. Watson played more than he had in years, first to spend more time with Edwards and then to raise awareness about ALS. He was in constant motion as he tried to help his friend find a cure.

Edwards died on the first day of the 2004 Masters. Watson played that day because he knew that's what Edwards would have wanted. After the round he said, "I felt like Bruce was with me."

Watson worked hard to rebuild his relationship with his father. He and Ray were so alike—stubborn, proud, conservative, the very cliché of men's men—and yet there was tension between them. Ray's heavy drinking had embarrassed Tom. At one point he forbade his father from attending his golf matches. Tom's drinking later in life and his public criticism of the Kansas City Country Club had driven the wedge deeper. Over the years, though, Ray quit drinking, Tom quit drinking, the two men worked through their differences.

"My father," Watson said in an unusually open moment, "is not an easy man. I never felt like anything I did was good enough. I'm sure that's a big reason why I became a champion. He is responsible for everything I achieved. But it hasn't been easy."

Father and son were in Hawaii for a golf tournament when Ray died of a heart attack. Tom was on the putting green when he found out. He told reporters, "Dad taught me the game. He didn't just teach me how to play. He taught me etiquette too. He said to me, 'Here's where you stand. You don't stand behind people. You keep quiet when somebody's trying to hit.' He loved the game. He gave me that love."

There were other relationships to mend. Watson's twenty-five-year marriage with Linda ended in a grueling divorce, putting distance between him and his two children, Meg and Michael. Slowly they came back together. Watson was as stubborn and difficult and principled as he'd ever been, but he developed a softer edge. He quit drinking.

"It was great to see a guy who had that problem, whose father had that problem, finally face it and fix it," Nicklaus says. "I was proud of him."

Nicklaus dealt with his own pain, none of it more heart-wrenching than in 2005, when his seventeen-month-old grandson Jake drowned in a hot tub. Jake was the grandson who hugged like he would never let go. "The hardest part is watching your children suffer," Nicklaus said. "It's a double whammy for a grandparent. That's just not supposed to happen."

When it happened, Nicklaus never wanted to play golf again. His son Steve felt differently. Golf, especially for his father, was too important to stop playing. Then one day, Watson called up Nicklaus and asked if he and Steve would like to play in the senior event in Kansas City; a special exemption had been given for Steve to play.

"Do you want to play in Kansas City?" Nicklaus asked his son.

"Sure, I'd love to play."

They went to Kansas City, and they stayed with Watson on his farm. They fished a lot, and the two great rivals talked—not so much about their tournaments together or the sadness they endured or the feelings about getting older. They just talked.

"We've known each other for so long," Nicklaus said, "that a lot can just go unspoken."

. . .

A couple of weeks later, Nicklaus played his final Open Championship. It was, fittingly, at St. Andrews, the birthplace of golf, the place where he had taken off his yellow sweater, a place that meant the world to him. He was paired with Watson for his last round. It could not have been any other way.

When the pair reached the 18th hole on Friday, it was clear that Nicklaus would not make the cut. Watson had a chance if he played a solid hole. They both hit their tee shots into the fairway and walked toward the green. Nicklaus looked into the crowd and smiled. Watson, so famously unsentimental, began to cry.

"Stop crying, Tom," Nicklaus ordered. "You still have some golf to play."

Watson nodded, and they kept walking. Watson did make his putt, and he made the cut. Then he left the stage to Nicklaus, who faced a fourteen-foot putt. He stalked it like the Nicklaus of old. "It didn't really matter," he recalled. "I knew wherever I hit it, the hole would move."

The ball rolled in and the Scottish crowd went mad one last time. Nicklaus gave a small smile, and Watson felt tears building in his eyes again.

"There," Watson said out loud, "is the greatest golfer who ever lived."

LOVE THE BAD BOUNCES

I asked him, "Tom, how do you win five British Opens?" He gave a little pause and said, "I love bad bounces." I looked at him kind of funny, and he said, "It was really clear to me when I looked around at other golfers that, you know, you can't handle bad bounces. But I can."

JOHNNY MILLER

The most compelling part of Watson's golf career is locked up in that word: *love*. He learned not only to accept the bad bounces but, against logic, to love them. He learned not only to endure but to love the rain and wind. "Bad bounces are part of golf," he says. "If you don't accept that . . ."

"Right," I say, "but you do more than accept that. You love it."

"Well, it's a challenge," Watson acknowledges. "I've always loved a challenge."

There's a classic *Twilight Zone* episode in which, after a degenerate gambler dies, he finds himself in the afterlife checked into a beautiful hotel. His closet overflows with perfectly fitted suits. Women find him irresistible. And he cannot lose any game he plays. Every time he spins the slot machine, it comes up sevens.

When he plays roulette, his number hits. He can't stop getting blackjack. After some weeks of this, he's utterly bored, and he screams at the man he presumes is his guardian angel that he doesn't belong in heaven.

"Whatever gave you the idea this is heaven?" the man replies. "This is the other place."

This is a theme Watson can relate to. Golf on sunny, windless days, those heavenly days for the rest of us, stopped appealing to him long ago. He wants to try shots he's never had to hit before. He wants to escape inescapable traps. He wants to face the sorts of predicaments that test his patience and his imagination and his resolve.

He was always good at handling difficult conditions. He had a toughness that other golfers lacked. Watson—and Nicklaus and Tiger Woods and pretty much every great golfer through the years—wants to face difficult conditions because he believes in his ability to overcome them. "Come on, Watson," he will say to himself in the howling wind or in foot-high rough. "Let's see if you're as good as you think you are."

Obviously it is a lot easier to love the bad bounces when you have Watson's game. But he thinks there's something in there for weekend golfers. "The best part of playing golf," he says, "is hitting great shots. And what gives you the opportunity to hit your greatest shots? Getting in some trouble."

"I was the kind of golfer who did not like bad breaks," Johnny Miller admits. "I think most golfers are like that. Tom was just different that way."

HOLE NO. 17

Watson heard a clear voice in his head when he returned to Turn-berry for the Open Championship the last time. "You can win this one, Watson," the voice said.

That voice had never left him. It was there in the early years, when he was unable to finish off tournaments. It was there during the glory years. It was there during the slump, and it was there as he grew old. The voice surfaced every time he had a good prac-tice session and spoke most clearly when he returned to a golf course where he had won a big tournament. The voice was not very realistic.

Watson was fifty-nine when he returned to Turnberry in 2009. He'd had his hip replaced only a few months earlier. He had not won a major championship in twenty-five years. "You can win this one, Watson," the voice in his head repeated.

It had been thirty-two years since the Duel in the Sun, thirty-two long years, and even the eternal Turnberry had reluctantly changed. The Turnberry of 1977 could not support 2009 golf. Golf clubs were so much more powerful. Golf balls soared higher and farther. Like all the grand old courses, Turnberry had to be stretched and pulled and reconfigured, like a house that has been outgrown.

Underneath, of course, this was still Turnberry, still that beautiful stretch of land by the Firth of Clyde on the west coast of Scotland. There were secrets in the dunes, riddles in the wind, mysteries that Watson alone understood.

"There's a spirit there that you have to experience to understand," said the mogul Donald Trump, who eventually would buy Turnberry. "There's something about Turnberry that is ancient, something that only people who live there truly understand. Tom understands it too."

No fifty-nine-year-old could win an Open Championship. Everybody knew that. The oldest man ever to win an Open Championship was Old Tom Morris, and he was just forty-six. The idea of Watson winning at fifty-nine was ludicrous.

Jack and Barbara Nicklaus were watching the golf coverage from Turnberry when they saw Watson with his caddie Neil Oxman. Their pairing was fitting. It was Oxman who, thirty-six years earlier, had suggested that his good friend Bruce Edwards go talk to that unknown golfer who looked like Huck Finn. Edwards had died five years earlier, and Oxman and Watson missed him terribly. When they were together, they felt a little of his spirit.

"Look!" Barbara said as she pointed at the television. Jack squinted and saw what caught her attention: Oxman was wearing a Nicklaus Golden Bear hat. It was a sign. They had to text Watson.

"Tom," Barbara wrote, "we love Ox's hat."

"It made us pay attention from the start," Nicklaus remembers.

Watson's first round at Turnberry in 2009 was like a dream in all those wonderful and unsettling ways of dreams. The wind was still. The course was defenseless. Every shot felt true. Every putt curled toward the hole. On the 1st, Watson hit a brilliant 9-iron to twelve feet and made birdie. On the 3rd, his twenty-foot birdie putt dropped to put him 2-under par. Oxman remembered thinking, "Hey, what's happening here?"

"You endure a lot of rough days," Watson would say, "so that every now and then you can have a good day." On the 10th hole, his gorgeous 6-iron shot settled three feet from the hole. He made that birdie to go 3-under par. On the 12th hole, he rolled in a fourteen-footer to go 4-under par. On the 17th, he made it 5-under with an easy birdie. Each of these holes was like an old friend.

At the end, all of Scotland seemed to be buzzing. Watson finished the day one shot off the lead. "It was," Oxman would say, "a perfect round of golf."

If anything, it was too perfect. Watson had led the U.S. Open after one round just months before Bruce died. He had a couple of good rounds at the Masters long after anyone saw him as a contender. But this round was different. This round was perfect. And perfect rounds, like sweet dreams, end abruptly when morning comes. In the sportswriting business, Watson's brilliant first round is called a "one-day story." As in "You better write about Tom Watson today because he won't be a story tomorrow."

"Can you keep doing this?" Watson was asked.

"Who knows?" he replied. "Why not?"

Nicklaus felt an unfamiliar jolt of excitement as he watched Watson play. It was unfamiliar because he rarely watched golf on television for more than a couple of minutes at a time. Other people playing just didn't interest him much. He never did like sitting still. He wanted to be flying somewhere for business, playing doubles tennis on his local Florida court, doing something with his family. But Watson contending at Turnberry fascinated him. Barbara asked if Watson could keep it up.

"Maybe," he answered. "He knows that course better than anyone. The key will be his putting."

Then Nicklaus remembered his last great run. That was at Augusta when he was fifty-eight. He made a charge on Sunday and moved all the way to the lead, though in time the other golfers caught him. It boggled everyone's mind except his own. In his own mind, he should have won that tournament.

"He can do this," Nicklaus decided. "But tomorrow will be harder than today."

The second day began for Watson as Nicklaus thought it might. The wind, so calm and friendly the day before, rushed in from the Firth. Watson made birdie on the 1st hole. On the 2nd hole, though, he hit his drive into heavy rough and made bogey. And it no longer felt like a dream.

Watson hit his second shot into a bunker on the 4th hole and made bogey. On the 5th, his drive died in the wind, and he made another bogey. On the 6th, his ball rolled into another bunker. Another bogey. On the 7th hole, he hit his second shot into the rough. He made bogey again. The huge crowd still milled behind him, but what they had hoped would feel like time travel instead had become that familiar and melancholy story of a man growing old. A few people began to break away to find a happier story.

Then something unexpected happened. Watson was playing with Sergio Garcia, one of golf's more emotional players.

Garcia had wondrous talent; when he first came on tour his touch around the greens and ability to hit brilliant shots when in trouble reminded observers of the young Tom Watson. But he felt jinxed. Every missed putt was a sign of doom. Every bad bounce convinced him that the golfing gods were against him. "This doesn't happen to other golfers," he moaned in those moments when things went bad. Watson, who liked Garcia, wished he could convince the young man that he was talented and blessed.

Now, though, Garcia was watching Watson's game deteriorate. And he spoke up. "Come on, old man!" he shouted. "You can do this! You're driving the ball well. You can do this!"

After that Oxman saw a noticeable shift in Watson's demeanor. He smiled that hard smile. On the 9th hole, he hit his second shot twenty feet from the flag. He looked the putt over quickly and then cracked the ball toward the hole. The putt dropped. He raised his arms to the cheering crowd. He had life yet.

Watson made another twenty-footer for birdie at the 11th. Rain began to fall, and he hit perhaps his worst shot of the back nine on the 16th hole, a 7-iron that flew over the green and settled some seventy feet away from the cup, setting up a very difficult two-putt. Watson made it in one.

"Oh my gosh!" Nicklaus yelled in Florida.

Then came the 18th hole, and Watson improbably was just one shot off the lead. His second shot barely rolled on the green; it was fifty-five feet from the hole. "I think Bruce is with us today," he said, and Oxman began to cry. Watson felt the tears in his own eyes, and people in the gallery who didn't even hear what Watson had said were crying too. The putt was a nasty twister, another difficult two-putt. Watson was not thinking about two-putts, though. He knocked in the crazy putt and walked off the green to the sound of impossible cheers. His name was on top of the leaderboard.

"It's your job, guys, to write the stories," he told reporters after his round. "My job is to make them."

Nicklaus was bouncing around the house; he could barely contain his excitement. Reporters wanted a statement. He sent one: "Hopefully he will forget his age and remember that he's Tom Watson. And Tom Watson knows how to finish."

Then he asked Barbara to send a text to Watson. Jack had no idea how to text. He was not especially interested in new technologies. He'd been lobbying the golf industry for years to go back to golf balls that didn't fly quite so far. Still, he had something to say to Watson. Barbara sent the first text: "Everybody's going to be giving you their best shot (you know that reference). But I know you can take it."

The "best shot" reference was to the Duel in the Sun. When it ended, Nicklaus had said, "I'm tired of giving it my best shot and not having it be good enough."

"What did getting that text mean to me?" Watson asks. "It meant everything. Especially because I know that Jack doesn't know how to text."

The wind at Turnberry shifted for the third round, and Nicklaus settled into his chair to watch. "Nobody's going to score well," he told Barbara. "All Tom has to do is shoot even par and he will be leading this tournament at the end of the day."

Watson was thinking along the same lines. The conditions were tough, and no golfer would be able to make up much ground if Watson played solid golf. So that's what he did. He teetered a little bit on the back nine but then made back-to-back birdies on the 16th and 17th to finish with a 1-over-par 71. He was alone in the lead.

Jack and Barbara cried during the round. Jack asked Barbara to send one more text: "Win one for us old guys. And make us all cry again."

The final day at Turnberry was a whirlwind of brilliant shots, poor shots, comebacks, tension—exactly what Nicklaus knew would happen. "The thing Tom will realize is that the golf course is not easy," he told reporters. "No matter what everybody else does tomorrow, they will make mistakes. He will too. His advantage is he knows that."

The course was a severe test; a fifteen- to twenty-mile-per-hour wind blew unpredictably. Watson lost his lead on the 1st hole, where he hit into a bunker and made bogey. A twenty-nine-year-old British golfer named Ross Fisher, who was carrying a beeper because his wife was due to deliver their child at any moment, made birdie to take a one-shot lead. The day would test all of them.

Watson hit his drive into the rough on the 2nd hole but salvaged par. On the 3rd, which was playing downwind, he did not follow one of his golf commandments—Overestimate the wind—and hit his shot over the green. He made his second bogey and fell down the leaderboard.

But Nicklaus was right: Watson's advantage was that he knew this would be a long and hard day. He could not win the tournament with a single shot. He also could not lose it that way. Fisher had a disaster at the 5th hole and fell out of the lead. He was replaced at the top by another British golfer, Lee Westwood, who made an eagle on the 7th hole. Many viewed Westwood as the best golfer never to have won a major championship.

All the while, Watson felt calm. This was how the day had to go. There would be multiple leaders, ups and downs, and he simply had to stay steady. He made a birdie on the 7th hole to pull within a shot of Westwood. He bogeyed the 9th hole to fall back two shots. Westwood bogeyed and the lead was one again.

In Florida, Nicklaus could not take his eyes off the television. The day was going just as he hoped. The leaderboard was turning and twisting—now a thirty-something Australian named Mathew Goggin worked his way to the top—but it did not matter. All of the other golfers would have to face a kind of turbulence that they had never felt before; there is nothing quite like being in contention for the first time at a major championship. Watson knew that feeling. He'd grown accustomed to it. When he birdied the 11th hole to move into a share of the lead, Nicklaus nodded. On the next hole, Watson's drive hit a woman in the crowd and ricocheted into the rough. He signed a golf glove for the woman, hit the ball onto the edge of the green, and saved his par. Nicklaus nodded again.

It is not quite right to say that the years melted off Tom Watson that afternoon in Scotland. He looked more or less his age. The wrinkles obscured the Tom Sawyer looks that writers once celebrated. Though he walked without a limp, the hip replacement slowed him down. And, more than anything, he kept leaving his putts short. He once rapped his putts harder than anyone; now he was not as sure. He was, in all ways, a man nearing sixty. And this was what made it all so wonderful.

When Watson made a bogey on the 14th hole, his ten-foot par putt slipping by the right side, he again fell behind by a shot. Then, almost immediately, Westwood bogeyed and they were tied. "Everyone was making mistakes," Watson later said. It was just as Nicklaus had foreseen.

At the 16th hole, Watson faced what seemed the pivotal moment of the day: a tricky four-foot putt for par. This was precisely the distance that had wrecked the latter part of his career. As a young man, he had knocked in four-foot putts without even thinking about them. At fifty-nine, making this four-foot putt seemed as easy as jumping over a canyon. He stood over the putt for the longest time while the people in the gallery, seeing his struggle, prayed for him. "Come on, Tom!" Jack and Barbara Nicklaus urged back home.

Watson made the putt, and it felt like the cheers were coming from around the world. He raced to the par-5 17th, the hole called "Lang Whack," where he had finally taken the lead from Nicklaus in the Duel in the Sun. He hit his drive into the rough. He hit his second shot over the green. He putted the ball back up to within a few inches of the hole. And then he made birdie. He led by one.

To win the Open Championship, he needed only a par on the 18th, a hole that had been renamed "Duel in the Sun" to commemorate what he and Nicklaus had done as younger men.

Already people were trying to put the story in perspective. Had there ever been anything like this in golf? No. How about in other sports? A forty-five-year-old George Foreman had become heavyweight champion. A fifty-nine-year-old Satchel Paige had pitched three good innings in a Major League Baseball game. Martina Navratilova won the Wimbledon mixed-doubles title at forty-six. The answer, obviously, was no. There had never been anything quite like this.

Watson stepped to the 18th tee and hit a magnificent drive

that rolled over the plaque in the ground that commemorated where his 1977 drive had landed. His ball was in perfect position, 189 yards from the flag. Golf fans around the world felt the tears forming in their eyes. Watson, though, saw clearly.

"I'm thinking eight-iron," Oxman suggested.

"So am I," Watson agreed.

Watson wanted to hit his shot 164 yards; this would land the ball on the front of the green and, after the roll, leave him with an easy two-putt to win the championship. To hit a shot 164 yards under normal circumstances, he would have used a 7- or 8-iron. But these weren't normal circumstances. The words of his English caddie Alfie Fyles echoed from 1977. "The way your adrenaline's pumping, Mister," Fyles had said as he handed Watson a 7-iron during the Duel in the Sun, two clubs less than he normally would hit.

Oxman later said that he would regret giving Watson that 8-iron for the rest of his life. But that came later. Watson hit his shot pure, and with the ball in the air he thought, despite himself, "I'm going to win the Open Championship." The ball looked gorgeous in the air. It hit the front of the green, bounced forward, and rolled fast. It rolled over the green into the fringe.

"Oh no!" Nicklaus shouted as he watched on television. "That shot was six inches away from being perfect."

Watson reached the green and saw that the ball was resting against a collar of grass. He had a choice to make. One of the great chippers in golf history, he could chip the ball. If he did, he would have a good shot of knocking it right next to the hole for an easy par and the Open victory. Then again, if he flubbed that chip he might find himself right back in the same spot.

His second option was to putt the ball; he had just successfully putted from off the green at the 17th hole. The advantage of putting was safety. He was not going to flub a putt. The disadvantage was distance control. He'd have a harder time getting the ball close.

In this moment, Watson asked himself, "What would Jack do?" Well, he decided, there was no question about that. Nicklaus would putt the ball. There's an old saying in golf that Nicklaus believed: Your worst putt will always be better than your worst chip. Watson had to give himself at least a chance to win the golf tournament.

So he putted, but not especially well. The ball rolled by and meandered to eight feet from the hole. On television, the broadcaster and Watson's close friend Andy North told America, "I think he's going to make this." That was North's heart talking. Watson's body language suggested he did not know how to make the putt. He walked around and studied it. As he stood over the ball unsteadily his pant legs fluttered in the wind. The young Watson would have rapped his putt at the hole with all the confidence in the world. The old Watson hit the ball tentatively. The young Watson would have made the putt or sent it rolling three feet by the cup. The old Watson left it short and right and nowhere near the hole.

All around the world a groan went up at once. Watson's bogey dropped him into a playoff with Stewart Cink. Though he put on a brave face, he was spent. For four days he had fought back the years, and now, all at once, he felt his age. He did not put up much of a fight in the playoff. Cink won it easily. And Watson, at age fifty-nine, finished second at the Open Championship. That in itself was remarkable. But it was not the ending anyone wanted.

Afterward Watson was surrounded by a distressed and miserable-looking press corps. "Hey, guys," he said. "It's not a funeral."

Back in Florida, Jack and Barbara sat on the couch and felt empty. "Heartbroken," Nicklaus later described the moment. "Heartbroken for Tom."

Watson put on a strong face, but deep down he too was heartbroken. In time, the Watson story would shift from a tearjerker to an inspiration. Look how close he had come. People on every continent wrote heartfelt letters to him. People in their fifties and sixties and older wrote that he had given them hope. Others wrote that Cink may have won the tournament, but Watson had won a piece of immortality; no one would ever forget how he played at Turnberry the last time.

Watson, though, did not want to hear any of that. He still saw things through a midwesterner's eyes. "Bottom line," he said, "I lost the Open."

He played over the final sequence in his mind again and again. Should he have hit a 9-iron instead of an 8? Maybe so. Should he have found a way to settle himself better before hitting that crucial final putt? Perhaps. More than anything he asked himself if he should have chipped that ball that went over the green. These were the thoughts raging through his mind as he sat in his hotel room in the minutes after he lost. That's when the phone rang. "I don't want to talk to anyone," he told his wife, Hilary.

But it was Nicklaus, so Watson picked up the phone.

"Tom," Nicklaus said, "I did something today that I have never done before. I watched a whole golf tournament on television."

"Thanks, Jack."

"You know . . . you won the golf tournament, Tom."

Watson shook his head. "What are you talking about? I didn't win the tournament."

"You beat everyone in the field," Nicklaus insisted.

"No, I didn't."

"Well, okay, you tied one." Nicklaus thought this might make Watson laugh. It did not.

"Yeah," Watson said, "and I lost to him in a playoff." He knew what Nicklaus was trying to do, but it wasn't helping. He felt his anger with himself growing again.

"Tom," Nicklaus continued softly, "you made us proud. How many fifty-nine-year-olds lead the Open Championship after two rounds? One, Watson: you. How many lead after three rounds? Only you, Watson. Only you. How many lead after four rounds? You."

Watson didn't reply. He just stared out the window into the Scottish countryside.

"You know, Tom, you played the eighteenth hole beautifully. You hit a perfect drive. You got unlucky on the second shot. And then you did the right thing putting that third shot. That was the right shot."

Watson perked up. "Was it?"

"Yes. That was the right shot. With a putter, you weren't going to lose the golf tournament. You might not win it, but you are not going to lose it. You chip there, you're bringing double bogey into play, and you have a chance to lose right there."

"Well," Watson said, "I'm glad you said that. But I goosed it."

"Yes," Nicklaus agreed, "and so would everybody else."

Watson let out a small laugh.

"I see it like this, Tom. With a chance to win the Open Championship, you hit a perfect drive. You hit a perfect second shot. You hit a smart third shot. And then . . . well, then you hit the putt just like any of us old guys would."

This time Watson laughed harder.

Later he said, "I still felt terrible, but I was beginning to come out of it. Jack had done something for me. I was thinking a lot about that third shot, that putt. Should I have chipped it? When the smartest golfer who ever lived tells you that you hit the right shot, that meant a lot to me. It still means a lot to me."

When Nicklaus was told that, he smiled. "Well, it was the right shot. You don't put yourself in position to lose. If you do that, you have a good shot of winning. It doesn't always work out. But that's your best shot."

CHASE THE SECRET

Every golfer has his own secret.

TOM WATSON

There isn't a secret to golf, of course. But no real player believes that.

JACK NICKLAUS

The worst thing that can happen to any golfer is to lose hope. One lousy round follows another, shots hook into the woods or slice into the water time after time, putts from three feet away skid short of the hole or roll five feet by. At some point the golfer starts to think that it will never get better. The promise of a new golf club or the next lesson fades. This is the time many golfers quit.

Nicklaus believes that this is precisely the time when golfers can play their best. "Golf is probably the easiest game in the world to quit at. But it's also the greatest game *not* to quit at."

"Why is that?" I ask.

"Because when you conquer the game again, when you hit good shots again, golf is an even greater game that it was before."

Watson agrees. The Secret, he says, is not one thing. All those lessons, all those ideas, they're all secrets. Golf has millions of them, and they change day after day. He chased the secret when he was playing well, and he chased the secret when he was playing lousy. He chased the secret when he was young and impetuous and somewhat liberal-minded. He chased the secret when he was older and hardened and staunchly conservative. He chased the secret so that he could beat his father, and he chased the secret when his father was gone. He chased the secret when he played Nicklaus at Turnberry as a young man and when he played Turnberry as an old man.

The chase has marked Watson's life. He admits to making many mistakes, on the golf course and off. But he never stopped trying to find the secret. That's what he's most proud of in his game. "There were times when I thought, 'I'm never going to find it,'" he says. "Those are the tough times. The key is to keep going, keep searching. The secret is out there. I'd say it's out there for every golfer. You just have to keep looking for it."

HOLE NO. 18

The most disappointing golf tournament of Watson's life was not, as you might think, when he lost to Cink in a playoff at the 2009 Open Championship. It happened at the same place, Turnberry, but it occurred fifteen years earlier, when he lost the Open Championship to Nick Price.

A look at the final scores would not suggest that Watson was close to beating Price; he shot a 74 on the final day and finished in eleventh place. But what the scores did not show was that Watson hit the ball better than anyone that week. In truth, he may have hit the ball better that week than he ever had in his life.

This was just a couple of months after he had found his Secret, just a couple of months after he had fixed the arc of his swing. All week he hit the ball exactly where he aimed. If he wanted to turn the ball left to right, he turned it left to right. If he wanted to move the ball right to left, he did that. He hit the ball high when he needed that shot, and he hit it low when that was required. After three rounds he was a shot off the lead even though he had missed, by his own estimation, at least ten putts he should have made. He missed two three-footers just on the back nine on Saturday; if he had made those he would have had the lead to himself.

"Hiccups," he called those missed putts after the round. "Those damned hiccups."

He told the press that he wanted the wind to blow hard in the final round; with a howling wind the tournament might come down to the player who hit the ball the best rather than the best putter. But the wind did not blow at all on Sunday, so the tournament came down to the player who putted the best. That was Nick Price. Watson still had a share of the lead as his back nine began, but then it all fell apart. He made back-to-back double bogeys when he badly missed two very short putts.

When it ended, Watson was inconsolable. He asked the question Ben Hogan had often asked in his later years: What use was it to hit the ball so well if he could not make any putts? What hope did he have of winning if the ball wouldn't go in the hole? He went to his hotel room and sulked.

The phone rang; it was Nicklaus. "Come on. Let's go get some dinner."

"No," Watson said, "I wouldn't be much company."

"Come on, get out of that room. Let's get some food."

"No," Watson said. "I can't." And he hung up the phone.

A few minutes later, Nicklaus's phone rang. "Okay," Watson said, "you're right. I'll meet you in the restaurant."

The four of them—Jack and Barbara, Tom and Linda—met in the dining room. They ate dinner and drank wine and told stories. They laughed a lot, especially Watson. The sun stays out late into the evening in Scotland that time of year, and he looked out the window and then looked at Nicklaus with a funny expression.

"Come on," he said, "let's go play the pitch-and-putt."

Next to the Ailsa Craig course at Turnberry was a lovely little par-3 golf course. It overlooked Ailsa Craig and the Firth and the countryside of Scotland. The four of them staggered out to the course and played golf as the sun was setting in the distance. They played as husband-and-wife teams and continued to play even after the sun was gone and it was dark all around them.

"Uh-oh," Nicklaus said, "Tom's got a five-footer. No chance he makes this."

Watson growled and made the putt.

"See how well you putt when you can't see the hole?" Nicklaus teased.

"You jerk," Watson responded, but he was laughing, they were all laughing, and in a life of wonderful shots and terrible ones, big victories and tough defeats, duels in the sun and the rain, they would both think of this as one of the happiest moments in their lives. What is the secret of golf? Well, as Hogan said, you have to dig it out of the dirt.

George Brown, the Turnberry Golf Course manager, lived in a house across the street. He heard laughter and went to see what the ruckus was. He gingerly approached the four trespassers playing golf in the dark.

Watson saw Brown first. He turned to Nicklaus. "Hey, Jack," he said as he pointed at the approaching man, "why don't you take care of this?"

ACKNOWLEDGMENTS

Years ago, during one of our countless conversations, I asked Tom Watson if he would ever want a book written about him. His answer was an unequivocal no. So when I first thought about writing this book, I did not expect him to care much for the idea. I sent him a letter explaining that I wanted to write a book about a rivalry and a friendship; he responded with a small card. Before I opened it, my wife, Margo, said, "Well, that's the shortest rejection note ever written."

Instead Watson wrote, "I will be happy to help you with this project any way I can." He was, as always, true to his word, and for that I am eternally grateful.

The man he chased, Jack Nicklaus, has been thoroughly kind to me for twenty-five years, though he is so kind in general he probably did not even notice. I thank him for the two dozen or so interviews through the years, and particularly for the last one, the longest ten-minute interview ever granted to a writer.

Thanks to Nick Seitz, who has been Tom Watson's longtime collaborator, and Howard Richman, who covered Watson skillfully as golf writer for *The Kansas City Star*. I interviewed or exchanged emails with more than one hundred people for this book and thank them all. Because I wanted the book to be thin and light, many of their names do not appear. I hope their spirit does.

I am indebted to my employers at NBC Sports and the Golf Channel, who were supportive of the project and helpful in securing me interviews with numerous golfers.

There are several people who helped give me insight into Turnberry, that glorious golf course at the heart of this book, beginning with Donald Trump and his assistant Rhona Graff. Richard Hall, the director of golf, took me around the course himself and introduced me to Turnberry's historian, Jack Boyd, who was especially helpful.

Thanks to my editors Jofie Ferrari-Adler and Jon Karp for seeing the possibilities of this book, and my lifelong agent and friend Sloan Harris for helping them see. I thank my family, my friends Mike Vaccaro, Tommy Tomlinson, John Garrity, Larry Burke, Michael Schur, Brian Hay, Jim Banks, and Dan McGinn, and especially Ian O'Connor, who wrote a fantastic book about the Nicklaus-Palmer rivalry that sparked an idea. I want to thank my wonderful research assistant Lindsay Crouch, who was impossibly efficient and a great sounding board.

Most of all, I thank my older daughter, Elizabeth, who wanted this book to be called "The Secret of the Club"; my younger daughter, Katie, who wanted me to acknowledge our dog, Westley; and my wife, Margo, who has been my secret through everything.

A NOTE ON SOURCES

Much of this book is based on my many interviews with Tom Watson and Jack Nicklaus, as well as other golfers, during my years as a columnist at *The Kansas City Star*. The play-by-plays and history of golf mainly come from the Associated Press and United Press International wire services and other newspaper accounts, along with the essential writing of Dan Jenkins, John Garrity, Michael Bamberger, and many other wonderful golf writers at *Sports Illustrated*.

A selected bibliography follows, but let me make special mention of Jack Boyd's *The Bonnie Links of Turnberry*, Michael Corcoran's *Duel in the Sun*, and John Feinstein's fine book about Bruce Edwards, *Caddy for Life*. I had many conversations through the years with Bruce, and I hope this book has some of his spirit.

SELECTED BIBLIOGRAPHY

Barrett, David. *Making the Masters: Bobby Jones, Clifford Roberts, and the Birth of America's Greatest Golf Tournament.* Skyhorse, 2012.

Boyd, Jack. *The Bonnie Links of Turnberry.* Turnberry Golf Club, 2004.

Clavin, Tom. *Sir Walter: Walter Hagen and the Invention of Professional Golf.* Simon & Schuster, 2005.

Corcoran, Michael. *Duel in the Sun: Tom Watson in the Battle of Turnberry.* Simon & Schuster, 2002.

Dodson, James. *American Triumvirate: Sam Snead, Byron Nelson, Ben Hogan and the Modern Age of Golf.* Knopf, 2012.

Dodson, James. *Ben Hogan: An American Life.* Doubleday, 2005.

Feinstein, John. *Caddy for Life: The Bruce Edwards Story.* Little, Brown, 2004.

Hogan, Ben, and Herbert Warren Wind. *Ben Hogan's Five Lessons: The Modern Fundamentals of Golf.* Touchstone, 1985.

Huber, Jim. *Four Days in July: Tom Watson, the 2009 Open Championship, and a Tournament for the Ages.* Thomas Dunne Books, 2010.

Nelson, Byron. *How I Played the Game.* Taylor Trade, 2006.

Nicklaus, Jack, and Ken Bowden. *Golf My Way.* Simon & Schuster, 2005.

Nicklaus, Jack, and Ken Bowden. *Jack Nicklaus: The Full Swing.* Golf Digest Books, 1984.

Nicklaus, Jack, and Ken Bowden. *Jack Nicklaus: My Story.* Simon & Schuster, 1997.

Nicklaus, Jack, and John Tickell. *Golf and Life.* St. Martin's Griffin, 2003.

Nicklaus, Jack, and Herbert Warren Wind. *The Greatest Game of All.* Simon & Schuster, 1969.

O'Connor, Ian. *Arnie and Jack: Palmer, Nicklaus and Golf's Greatest Rivalry.* Houghton Mifflin, 2008.

Penick, Harvey, and Bud Shrake. *Harvey Penick's Little Red Book: Lessons and Teachings from a Lifetime of Golf.* Simon & Schuster, 2002.

Richman, Howard. *All Things Golf: Lessons, Thoughts, Tips, Reminders and Memories from Stan Thirsk.* Kansas City Star Books, 2004.

Watson, Tom, and Frank Hannigan. *The Rules of Golf.* Pocket Books, 1999.

Watson, Tom, and Nick Seitz. *Getting Up and Down.* Golf Digest Books, 1987.

Watson, Tom, and Nick Seitz. *The Timeless Swing.* Atria Books, 2011.

Watson, Tom, and Nick Seitz. *Tom Watson's Getting Back to Basics.* Pocket Books, 1992.

Watson, Tom, and Nick Seitz. *Tom Watson's Strategic Golf.* Pocket Books, 1993.

Wind, Herbert Warren. *Following Through: Herbert Warren Wind on Golf.* HarperPerennial, 1995.

ABOUT THE AUTHOR

JOE POSNANSKI is National Columnist for NBC Sports. He was a senior writer at *Sports Illustrated*, where he was named National Sportswriter of the Year by the Sportswriters and Sportscasters Hall of Fame. Before joining *SI*, he was a columnist for *The Kansas City Star* and was twice named the best sports columnist in America by the Associated Press Sports Editors. His books include *The Soul of Baseball*, *The Machine*, and *Paterno*, which was a #1 *New York Times* bestseller. He lives in Charlotte, North Carolina, with his wife, Margo; his daughters, Elizabeth and Katie; and their dog, Westley.